Reviews

"10 Steps... is an inspiration and an invaluable handbook for first-time and mid-level managers in both small and large companies. Many of these managers are puzzled by the very same challenges they face in their day-to-day work and life. The book provides great down-to-earth and ready-to-apply advice that can only come from true experiences. The concepts of the virtual box and "win, win, win"... are truly inspirational and original. It is a brilliant book!"

-- Tom Lu, Director of Engineering, Hewlett-Packard

This book reveals a step-by-step pathway for career advancement. It presents an integrated approach about virtual position- a paradigm shift in viewing your current position and future career path, training yourself before you really get the position, and preparing you for thinking to action for the next level. It's a great resource I would like to recommend to all my friends and colleagues.

-- Sharon Wan, Ph.D., Principal Software Development Manager, Microsoft Corp.

"A hard-to-find practical handbook that can help junior to mid-level managers to advance their career. A must-read!"

-- Henry Zhang, VP Operation, Chuwa America.

This is an awesome book guiding people in different fields to successful career. The concept of virtual box is especially novel and practical. I feel pulled into every story and naturally engaged in the follow-up exercises. I strongly recommend this book to everyone who is or will be climbing up the career ladders. You will be surprised at how much practical mentoring you can get from this book!

-- *Michelle Xu, software engineer*

I wish I had read this book when I started my career. Elizabeth and Pat masterfully distill the invaluable lessons that they learned from their successful careers into practical techniques and inspiring stories. Read this book, get a jump start on your career!

-- *Adrian Ng, Software Engineer, Oracle*

As a recent college graduate in today's tough economy, Elizabeth's book provides me with many useful insights and tools regarding the professional world. It's a must read for anyone like myself fresh on their way into their first career or someone ambitious looking to make their next big leap.

-- *Zhenni Wu, Student, UC Berkeley*

I wish my mom taught me these steps!

-- *John Zhang, Engineer from Silicon Valley*

Myths of the Promotion

10 Steps to a Successful Career

Elizabeth Xu, PhD.
Patricia Zimmerman

ISBN 978-1-937489-99-1

Library of Congress Control Number: 2012910877

Copyright © 2012 by Elizabeth Xu & Patricia Zimmerman

Published in 2012 by Elizabeth Xu & Patricia Zimmerman.

Printed in the United States of America

To

Lou Shaffer, our success is your legacy.

Also, to our students for their future success.

Have a great
Career!

Contents

Preface

A Journey Started in 2005

Ray asked me to give a talk at Santa Clara City Library in 2005. "What should I talk about? I would rather talk about something useful for the audience than about myself." "How about some fundamental steps to help other people build a successful career?" he said. I put together my 10 steps presentation and went over it with my mentor Pat, the winner of the national Jefferson and Kennedy Awards for volunteering and mentoring. To my surprise, over one hundred professionals came with questions such as: "I did a great job, why didn't I get a promotion? Why did I get laid off?" They wanted to learn how to control their destiny. These 10 steps resonated with them very well. They loved the seminar!

Invitations to speak at different groups continuously came. Pat and I conducted seminars and classes of various lengths. We have spoken to a few thousand professionals since 2005, and 40+ big companies and prestigious universities such as Google, Microsoft, Hewlett Packard, Yahoo, Cisco, Berkeley, George Washington, Santa Clara and Stanford University. Our students set up our blog at www.ElizabethXu.com in 2008 and asked us to offer the class at Stanford University in late 2010.

Stanford University accepted our class proposal for the Fall 2011 quarter. Pat and I successfully delivered the content of the book to 50 students. The class was well received. 60% of our students rated the class "Excellent and extremely useful", 40% of the students rated it "Good class and very helpful." Many students wrote thank you emails and encouraged us again to publish it as a business book ASAP. They wanted to use it as a career handbook.

This book is the designated textbook for our 2012 Fall Stanford class and will be the textbook for all our future classes and seminars.

Ten Steps to a Successful Career

Your career development has become your own responsibility in this ever-changing talent market. Global corporations no longer provide in-depth career development programs. Instead, they recruit talent from each other. This book will teach you how to build a successful career across multiple companies and industries, achieve your goals and advance your position in this super competitive global talent war.

This book will provide you with ten systematic steps extracted from great leaders in the industry and authors' real corporate executive experiences. The virtual position concept is original and paradigm changing for professionals to advance their career from individual contributors to mid-level managers and then to executive positions.

This book will completely change your mindset and your understanding in career advancement. These ten actionable steps will assist you in refining your career vision, building realistic goals, developing feasible plans and executing them flawlessly. Also discussed is how to create an effective professional brand and network, how to collaborate and influence others as well as how to build and lead a successful team. These ten steps will help you to develop a heightened business understanding and refine your important leadership skills.

A Wanted Handbook and Textbook

After receiving numerous inquiries about detailed training material, Pat and I started to write this book in late 2008. From an anonymous survey, conducted with our students, the following topics kept appearing as extremely helpful to their careers:

• Practical, systematic and easy-to-follow steps for regular people to build an extraordinary career

• Paradigm shift in elevating thinking and daily practice using virtual positions

• Best practices in day-to-day execution that provide shortcuts to accelerate career success

• Career branding methodology

• Business networking and mentoring

- Defining and catching opportunities to realize career goals

Our students found these topics, along with the rest of the 10 steps, to be very different from distinctive career success stories and advice. These steps are practical and useful in their daily work. They are confident these steps can accelerate their career.

How Does this Book Work

We expect our readers to use our book as a handbook at their workplace, understand the rules of career advancement, conscientiously follow these 10 steps to build their career, always look two levels up, build higher level thinking, business understanding and get ready for next level jobs.

We give homework at the end of each chapter as a review and means to practice the advice given in the chapter. With practice, you will be on the fast track to a successful career.

Learn, practice and teach!

Win, Win, Win!

Acknowledgments

We want to thank the many people who brought their skills and dedication to the completion of this book. This book could not have been written without the feedback of our students at Stanford, Berkeley, CAAEN, MTJA and NAAPSF Associations.

Next we want to thank the many reviewers who questioned our thoughts and corrected our mistakes: Robert Eaton, Yan Yang, Adrian Ng, Crystal Kung and YunYun Jiang. We love the cover designed by Michael and Hass Lunsford. Many thanks to Sue Chen for taking our manuscript and making it into a real book.

Special thanks go to Elizabeth's husband William and her sons Alex and Joey who lived through the birth and editing of this endeavor. Elizabeth also would like to thank her in-laws Mr. and Mrs. Li who have taken care of her two children since their birth. They helped the young family tremendously when she was teaching during weekends and evenings.

Now let's explore the myth of the promotion.

1

Understanding Yourself

Why Me First

The first step in building a successful career starts from understanding one important person - you. Without understanding yourself, you are fighting a battle without knowing your troops, weapons and resources. When you do understand yourself, you can identify your true life desires and goals as well as you can utilize your strengths to reach those goals. You can better understand and influence others. Furthermore, you will truly know how to work with, communicate with, inspire others and build meaningful relationships.

Understanding yourself is the fundamental and hardest first step, because you cannot see yourself externally, you only can get external validation from other people: the people you trust, people you do not trust, people you love and even people you hate.

Validations from these people are vastly different and contradictory; they are good references but not a solid base for you to build your career upon.

It is very hard to get a real view of yourself when you live in an ever changing and biased world. We live with that person we see in the mirror every day. It is human nature to be self-centered and love oneself. Most people who are willing to live in a self-filtered fantasy world unconsciously reject other people's perspectives in order to protect such a fantasy land in their own minds. However, in some extreme cases, people who have low self-esteem can only see their weaknesses. They are living in a dark critical self-constructed cave in their mind and can hardly see any of their prior successes and strengths. Highly accomplished people are critical of themselves as well. These people also must learn to love themselves before they can really learn to like others and work with others.

Perception is Reality

In 2003, I was on the path to be promoted to a director position. William, the SVP of Engineering, asked me to talk to my boss' peers. That was one of the most frightening events and also one of the best things that ever happened to me. Everyone I talked to taught me something useful. I was surprised with the best advice I got from my boss' peers. Wade, the VP of Application Engineering shared an excellent story with me.

Wade was an avid golfer and a very confident leader. He studied golf techniques and practiced whenever he had time. One day he reached a plateau. He hired an excellent coach to help him. The coach told him that he was moving his arms incorrectly. He refused to believe the coach. The following weekend the coach videotaped his movements and sat him down to watch the tape together. Wade watched and his jaw dropped. His coach was right, he waved his club a few inches lower and 30 degrees from the direction he thought he did. Instead of arguing with his coach, he accepted the coach's advice and practiced hard. His golfing skills improved significantly in a few short weeks.

Everyone has two reflections. One reflection is inside you, how you think, reason and make decisions. The other reflection is outside of you, the perception others have of you. Perception is truth to the person who perceives it. You cannot say a person's perception of you is not true because it is true to him. We are not always very truthful with ourselves; we filter out information, only believing what we want to believe. So the problem is - the disconnection between the inner you and how others perceive you. That disconnection is the plateau that blocks your career progress.

A Virtual Box - Everyone is Different

Let us construct a model that can help you visualize every aspect of the true you, to help you understand yourself systemically.

A virtual box consists of six facets. Each facet represents one aspect of you; it can help you understand your drive, why you think, reason, and act in certain ways.

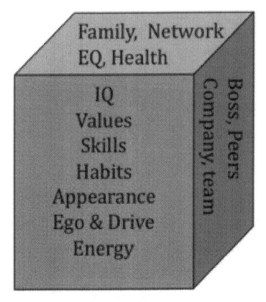

A Virtual Box represents a person

Facet one includes the qualities you have when you are born. These include your IQ (Intelligence Quotient), physical attributes, ego and drive. These qualities are within you waiting for you to develop them to the maximum.

Facet two includes the qualities learned while growing up. They include your values, willingness to take risks or your aversion to take risks.

Facet three is the quality and skills that you developed yourself such as: EQ (Emotional Intelligence Quotient), physical appearance, execution ability, healthy living habits, work habits and communication skills.

Facet four includes your family and social environment, friends and social network.

Facet five is your daily work environment, bosses, peers and employees.

Facet six includes your business relationships (clients) that provide opportunities as well as challenges.

Everyone lives in such a virtual box: the box has different shapes defined by various qualities and factors. We think through our issues, make and execute our decisions, and react to the external world from this virtual box. As you explore and define the virtual box, you will get to know that important person – you.

Values and Beliefs

The first version of values and beliefs was installed by your parents in your childhood. These change over time as you gain your own experiences. Values and beliefs are the standards in your mind for your decisions and actions. Behavior is the reflection of your values. Under extreme pressure, people usually revert back to their first version. I believe your fundamental values were established by the time you were ten years old. You might be able to understand people deeply by tracing back what happened in the world or their life by the time they were ten years old. However, values can be changed by dramatic life events later in life. Career growth is more organic when you are working for a company which has the same values as yours. When changing jobs, you need to look at the company and manager's values; always remember you are hiring a company as well as the company is hiring you.

Visions and Dreams

Visions are the way people see things in the future regardless of how things appear currently. Dreams are wishes and aspirations. Some dreams are not practical and some are. Visions and dreams excite people and inspire them to work hard to fulfill these visions and dreams. They encourage people to take big risks and build extraordinary businesses.

Pessimism kills dreams. It destroys dreams by exaggerating challenges and sucking positive energy from people. People are defeated before they even start the journey. A journey without dreams and visions is doomed to failure. A life without dreams is not exciting.

Robert Kennedy is quoted as saying: "Some people look at the world and say why. I look at the world and say why not." People who say "why not" are the inventors, they first have a dream and then make it a reality.

A leader must be able to form visions and dreams, instill them in his team and re-invent them constantly to keep the team motivated to strive for the best. They must remove pessimism from their team.

Physical and Mental Health

Many successful executives cultivate extraordinary physical and mental health to withstand the extreme pressure and demanding schedule required by their positions.

Many executives do exercise regularly (at least 45 minutes x 5 days per week) to improve their physical strength, energy level, release stress and eliminate burnout. They also have other ways to release stress and stay afloat mentally, such as: faith, strong values, mentors, support groups and strong family ties. Leaders constantly reinvent themselves by continuously looking for new ideas and using best practices.

Leaders must have the ability to excite people, simplify situations and make priority calls as well as to calm people down. It takes great mental strength to sort through complex situations under huge pressure. Mentally unstable leaders will oscillate organizations and dissipate positive energy and productivity.

IQ and EQ

IQ (Intelligence Quotient) is one way to measure one's intelligence. IQ is a score derived from several tests designed to access a person's intelligence. EQ (Emotional Intelligence Quotient) describes an ability, capacity, or skills to perceive, assess and manage the emotions of one's self, of others, and of groups. Both IQ and EQ can be developed. You can become an outstanding individual contributor only with high IQ and low EQ, however, we live in a collaborative world where only a high IQ cannot make you a successful leader. Although a high IQ is desirable, a high EQ is mandatory for a leadership position.

Ego and Drive

The Google dictionary defines ego as " a person's sense of self-esteem or self-importance." It also defines ego as "the part of the mind that mediates between the conscious and the unconscious and is responsible for reality testing and a sense of personal identity." However, ego is usually used in a negative way, as "the overly high opinion of oneself" in society. A healthy ego is not egotism or an egocentric way of talking and thinking about yourself, but it provides energy and keeps you more optimistic toward setbacks. Ego forces you to meet challenges and overcome obstacles.

Personal drive is the fire in the belly, the burning desire to be successful. It drives you toward your goals to the level your values permit.

One of the most important leadership traits is pursuing excellence. Steve Jobs, founder of Apple, was one the best examples of pursuing excellence and elegance in every product his team built. Personal drive and ego work together to drive oneself to do a better job today, outperforming what one accomplished yesterday.

Habits and Skills

Good habits are like a well-maintained engine. They will keep you going subconsciously without any additional effort. Turn best practices into habits. This will simplify your life and make you a more predictable and easy to follow leader. Good parents help their children cultivate good habits at a young age, good habits such as exercising regularly, eating a good diet, keeping promises and treating other people nicely and with integrity.

Once a practice becomes your habit, it is part of your muscle memory, you automatically do it without thinking. It is hard to forget and ignore, just like it is hard to unlearn how to ride a bike.

Skills are your tools. Our ever-changing world calls for new tools and you have to prepare for it. Investing money and time to learn these new skills and keeping you up-to-date with the trend is as important as eating food every day. Skills at different levels are different. Learning next level skills in advance will help you understand more about your business and prepare you for next level career advancement opportunities.

Appearance

When you act like a leader, talk like a leader and dress like a leader, you will get better career advancement opportunities.

One of my close college friends once said, "You are responsible for your appearance after you turn thirty. Your parents are no longer responsible for your look." The day we entered college, we started our maturing process, just like a newly bottled wine acquires its sophisticated taste over time.

Appearance is not only about external looks, your inner intelligence, confidence, leadership capability, communication skills, professional way of handling crises exude beyond the skin surface and high quality business suits. How you treat others, how you present yourself and treat your customers are also part of your appearance. Dressing for success is good advice but building your inner strength at the same time is even more important.

Family

Your family gave you your first version of values. Your family members have affected your life as you have theirs since you were in the womb. A loving family is the safe haven on which you can rely. They support you emotionally. In most cases, they are also the reason you are working hard. You want to earn the pride of your parents while providing a better life for your children. A good trusting relationship with your family provides you with security when you start to build relationships in the business world. Business best practices also can be applied to your family life, such as trust and positive reinforcement.

President Obama's family play a game called "Roses and Thorns" at their dinner table. They each take turns talking about good things (roses) and challenges (thorns) that happened that day. They share their excitement and concerns with each other, encouraging each other to manage their challenges positively. Children learn so much from this simple daily family activity. They get a preview of the real business world and the attitude their parents have toward low points. No wonder many executive's children become leaders quickly and naturally. It becomes part of their family muscle memory. They prepare their children to engage in the real world. On the other hand, sitting in front of the TV eating dinner teaches children to be passive, watching the world playing in front of their eyes. They are not participating in life.

Many businesses prefer to hire executives who have stable family lives. Divorce and affairs are destructive events distracting executives from their business commitments. One CEO of an executive recruiting firm said his firm stays away from such candidates because hiring companies do not want to deal with extra distractions.

Bosses, Peers, Employees

You are working for your bosses and your company, it is more than okay to prepare a presentation for your boss and prepare him to give the presentation to his bosses on behalf of your team. Your job is to make your boss as successful as possible. Working well with your peers also helps your boss to be successful.   However, I assume that your boss is totally in line with company priorities. Never blame your boss for not taking care of your career because you are the sole owner of your own career.   However, as a leader, if you want to have a strong team, you must identify potential stars and develop them.   Discovering the hidden talents of your employees and helping them to develop those talents is our responsibility as leaders.

Customers

Customers pay your bills. It is necessary to add value to your customers' businesses and lives, or your business will not succeed. You need to listen to their needs and build products according to their requirements. Do not waste your time telling them why you cannot provide the service they requested, instead, spend your time to meet their needs. Trusting relationships with customers brings reoccurring business. Your customer is always the number one priority for your company, so understanding your customer is also your top priority.

Network

Networking is so important to your career that an entire chapter, Chapter 8, is devoted to it. A well-connected network will give you opportunities and the talent you need for your excellent team. A supporter within your company who recognizes your passion, talent and experience can accelerate your career unexpectedly by providing you unknown opportunities that fit your experience, furthermore, your supporter might tailor some opportunities to fit into your qualifications to expand his team's bench strength.

Out of the Box Thinking

One critical leadership quality is out of the box thinking. How does one think out of the box? Just get out of your own virtual box!

No one can pull ideas out of thin air. You must have a frame of reference. Construct as many different virtual boxes in advance, build virtual boxes for your boss, peers, customers, parents, spouse and even for your children. Fly into the appropriate virtual box and think as if you are the owner of that virtual box. The magic will happen! You will see a unique perspective and come up with fresh ideas. It will help you with branding new product ideas, organizational ideas and even gift ideas for holidays! You integrate your experience and ideas with these fresh perspectives and elevate them into great ideas and generate strong synergy with others. Your ability in collaboration will make you the natural leader of the group. Your result is multi-fold.

It takes courage to step out of your own box, if you are a courageous person, you will be open to other people's ideas. At the end of the day, it is not about whose idea got chosen, it is about how to work with others to accomplish what you cannot achieve

How to Improve your EQ

To improve your EQ or EI (http://en.Wikipedia. org/wiki/Emotional intelligence), the ability to identify, assess, and manage your own emotion, other's emotion, or a group's emotion), you must first understand yourself thoroughly, then you can understand others better. The assumption is that everyone is different. Everyone is motivated differently, reasons differently and reacts differently even to the same event. You must first recognize the differences, accept the differences, work with differences, then appreciate differences and lastly value these differences. Only the person who can really utilize human differences at levels above their own can truly and accurately capitalize on the true value of human resources for their business.

How Do you Internalize Human Differences

Your own virtual box is the base to differentiate yourself from the rest of the world. Let us look at all six facets of your virtual box, weave your own self-understanding into your base virtual box.

Systematically compare your facets with others, such as your managers or business associates, understand their values, motivation, priorities, strengths, obligations and limitations from all six facets. Try to understand why you made certain decisions and why others made different decisions. These decision points provide data to calibrate these virtual boxes you construct for people around you. You will know what decisions were made and why these decisions were made, therefore you can predict future decisions better.

A simple task we ask our students (from workshops and seminars) to do is to construct a virtual box for their manager. Try to make a decision on a real issue from your boss' box each day. Then compare with the actual decision your manager made. The closer these two decisions become, the more you understand your manager. If you practice this simple task and constantly analyze the differences with real people, your assessments get more accurate over time. Then you have more control of your own emotions and can better assess other people's emotions. You have successfully improved your EQ and can better collaborate with others.

When you sit back and look at decisions and virtual boxes objectively and calmly, it opens up your mind to understanding why certain decisions were made. These decisions were based on information that was available to your boss at the time, but not necessarily available to you. Nothing evil or conspiratorial was behind these decisions. In many instances, you felt decisions were made from a vacuum, you were excluded from the decision making process. It is normal business practice not to consult everyone in the organization when making strategic decisions. So do not take it personally. However, communicating facts, data and solutions at the right time is the most effective way to influence decisions.

Keeping an open line of communication between you and your boss is important in many ways. It helps you understand each other better, as well as builds trust and respect.

Quiz: Are you Vocal Enough During Meetings?

Many of our students complain about not getting enough visibility. Are you vocal enough or are you just sitting in silence during meetings?

Try this simple test, which is well liked by our students:

1) Do you prepare a question before a meeting? No: 0, Yes: 1

2) Do you prepare a solution or a suggestion to problems to be discussed at the meeting? No: 0, Yes: 1

3) Do you ask questions during the meeting? No: 0, Yes: 1

4) Do you offer to make presentations at the meeting? No: 0, Yes: 2

5) Do you summarize or re-phrase other's points so as to understand what they say? No: 0, Yes: 2

6) Do you offer to write meeting minutes? No: 0, Yes: 1

7) Do you publish your opinions, results and papers? No: 0, Yes: 3

If you score 0-5, you are not vocal enough.

If you score 5-8 you are okay, but there is room for improvement.

If you score more than 8, you are vocal enough.

You can take the following action items to become more vocal during business meetings:

1) Prepare 1-5 questions for your next meeting; ask at least 2 of them. Write the meeting minutes for yourself.

2) Write down the best questions you heard from the meeting, prepare to use them in future meetings.

3) Discuss one suggestion before a meeting with 1-2 key players at the meeting; propose one suggestion or solution at the meeting. If you get positive interaction, observe people's reaction.

4) Read the meeting agenda, research related topics, prepare a few discussion points and supporting data.

What you Do Today Defines your Tomorrow

We all saw the catastrophic economic meltdown in 2008 and expected the long winter ahead of us. Many people lost their jobs and many lost hope in rapid career growth in the near future. What can we do in this situation?

Companies look for a winning strategy to survive in this roller coaster business environment. They revise their business plans and redefine processes.

This same strategy applies to all working professionals who run their careers as a business. They should re-evaluate and re-plan their careers, redefine current daily tasks to be more competitive and gain the ability to win when the market turns around.

What we do today defines what we become tomorrow. Transformation starts today and carries through each day whenever you decide to do things differently and more strategically.

Let us first understand what we do today. Log your activities for a whole week and classify your activities into the following categories:

Short term

1) Daily operational short term tasks

2) Temporary assignments

3) Tactical meetings

4) Routine jobs

Long term and strategic

1) Networking and mentoring

2) Learning new skills and building new strengths

3) Understand emerging technology and industries

4) Write white papers and summaries about your product and build your portfolio

5) Design and build your personal brand

6) Establish processes and automate your business operation

If you spend less than 20% of your time on long term and strategic activities, you must increase your investment in this category.

If you spend more than 20% of your time on long term and strategic activities, but you have not achieved your expected result, examine your goals and validate your strategy to reach such goals.

Log your time again one week per month, map your actual activities to your goal, measure the results and make it part of your routine.

Define yourself, start the transformation process today, and you will become the new person you are wishing to be in the near future.

Homework

1.   To understand your daily activities, for next 7 days - log your time and activities, create a time map. Eliminate unimportant and not urgent time-wasting activities.

2.   Write down the most dramatic events in your life, and the impact of these events to your life.

3.   Write down the three people who influence you the most and how you have changed because of their influence.

4.   Write down your values: people, things and principles that matter the most to you.

5.   Write down twenty friends and business relationships.

6.   Construct the virtual box in your mind.

7.   Analyze one of your decisions from your box per day, ask yourself why did you make such a decision, what facet of the box influenced your decision?

8.   Measure yourself on

- Peace of mind
- Big heart

- Elevated view
- Collaborative working style
- Health
- Personal drive

9. Build a virtual box for yourself.

10. Build a virtual box for your manager and two levels up.

11. Build a virtual box for one of your most important family members.

12. Turn a best practice into a new habit.

2

Elevating your Position

Look One Level Up - Help your Manager be Successful

The first week I started working at IBM, Pat advised me "look one level up." Pat suggested that I should always help my manager become more successful. Looking one level up means using my manager's priorities as my own and working on the most important tasks for my group, not just my own assignments.

That is easier said than done. We all deal with prioritization everyday - both in our work and personal lives. Which tasks should be considered more important and given more resources than others? Should you help your team be successful first or work on your own tasks first? Actually, the real question should be, "As a team which task is more strategic and important to the success of the group and the company?" When your team's priorities override your own priority, you are truly representing the team. And you will earn the right way to make priority calls - making decisions for your team. Talk to your manager to confirm group priorities then change your priorities and assignments to support the group goal. This will make you a more successful individual and a rising leader.

Look Two Levels Up – Get your Manager Promoted

How do you make your manager more successful and get him promoted? Remember, your manager's team is one level up so your 2nd line manager governs your manager's group priority. If you truly want your manager to be successful in his group, you have to understand two levels up. By that we mean you need to understand the priorities and business objectives two levels up so you can help your manager support your 2nd line manager's objectives. You should find solutions that help your manager's team and his peers' groups make his manager's organization successful. Use your strengths to compensate for your managers' weaknesses, give him credit and make your manager successful.

Win, Win, Win

I heard the term "location, location, location" for the very first time when I was hunting for my first house. No surprise at all, because I did not grow up in the United States and had no clue about how to select a house to buy.

What does this expression using three "locations" really mean? A curious person, as I have always been, asked many realtors and got many interesting answers. Most of them told me that three repeating locations mean that location is very important. My interpretation from my house hunting experience is:

1) Location: which city you want to raise your family in and what kind of life style does it provide

2) Location: What street you want to live on, small court close to highway or close to school, what kind of convenience it provides to your daily life

3) Location: the orientation/direction of your house, facing east, south, floor plan, size of the lot, plus some other considerations depending on your culture and the comfort level it provides.

When I had these three locations in mind, my decision was much easier. We "won the war" of buying our first house and we are proud of our decision.

When it comes to your career, many people hear "win, win, win" the very first time. Win-win is well understood: two parties try to construct a business solution beneficial to both parties.

What's "win, win, win"?

1) Win: Your company wins, your decisions and solutions must support your company's vision and strategy, help to execute it flawlessly.

2) Win: Your boss wins, you have to be a team player to support your boss' goals, working well with your peers and his peers to make your boss' team successful.

3) Win: Your people win! Provide leadership, build trust and give credit to your people; you need to enable them to win as a team.

Of course, you help all three parties win legally and also never compromise your personal integrity and values. When all three parties win, you will win the war of achieving a successful career and you will be proud of your career decisions and actions.

Is your View Grand and Elevated Enough?

Building a successful career is more about building a deeper and more sophisticated understanding towards your business, the organization and your team than about building skills and experiences. No matter what you have accomplished in the past, your understanding about business and organizations has to continuously elevate to the next levels before you advance to these levels.

Career growth starts as your understanding and view of the external world grows and expands. That view is the base where you form your vision, strategy and executable plans.

You can only get what you can see. Seeing problems, thinking through solutions and solving problems at higher levels certainly make you an obvious succession candidate. Senior management always looks for such candidates who show growth potential. The potential is proportional to the depth and width of your business understanding and how big the picture you can see and internalize; the level at which you are thinking about business issues.

Think Like an Executive

If you do not think like an executive, just dress like, look like and talk like an executive, you are only an actor from a show reciting scripts. Would you hire Michael Douglas as your executive for his outstanding performance? Absolutely not!

How do you think at the level to which you want to be promoted?

Virtual Positions Ready to Fly In

How do you gain insight about the positions you want to grow into? Construct a virtual position that represents the position that interests you.

Create an array of virtual positions that interest you. These virtual positions are ready for you to fly into at any time:

- View issues from these virtual positions

- Construct solutions and suggestions from these virtual positions

- Carry out meaningful conversations with the real owners of these positions

However, you cannot execute from these virtual positions. It is like the stock market games, you can practice and experience a stormy market, but you do not have real currency to purchase real stocks, you do not either gain or lose any real money. But you gain tremendous insights into the process.

How to Construct Virtual Positions

Every position comes with four basic attributes:

1) Responsibilities

2) Visibility

3) Resources

4) Reward

You may gain partial visibility by observing and calibrating your information continuously. You may assume some responsibility by volunteering and helping out. If you align yourself to the highest priority tasks in your organization, you will gain great insight, some responsibility and resources. This also helps you build a network.

We are not trying to clone that position; therefore, clear understanding of the responsibility and partial visibility will be enough for you to construct the virtual position. Discussions with the real owners of these positions will calibrate your accuracy.

My friend Jane likes to talk about her younger brother Bob, who is an accomplished business owner. Bob lived with Jane and her husband when he was in graduate school. He talked about his dream business in such detail every day; he was almost a virtual CEO of his future business. Bob talked about failures and successes of similar businesses he had heard or read about related to his dream business. Jane felt that Bob started his business when he was in graduate school, five years earlier than the actual start date.

What kept Bob going? Future rewards, not just financial rewards but also his accomplishments and realization of his career potential.

Jane first joked about her brother's dream. Later on, when Bob's dream became more vivid and exciting, Jane started to believe in him. Bob filled his virtual position with real details; he became a more real CEO every day!

A Virtual Position at your Manager's Level

Let us first construct a special virtual position to help you step into your manager's situation. Collect detailed information about your manager in the six facets:

Facet one: IQ, physical attributes, energy level, ego and drive

Facet two: Values, principles and willingness to take risks

Facet three: EQ, physical appearance, execution ability, healthy living, work habits and communication ability

Facet four: Family and social environment, friends and social network

Facet five: Daily work environment, bosses, peers, and employees

Facet six: Business relationships (clients) that provide opportunities as well as challenges

Once you understand your manager in the above six facets, a virtual box is ready for you to step into and allow you to think as your manager. Once you are in that virtual box, you understand and respect him as a real person, not just a figure of authority; you do know why he made certain decisions.

Let us deploy your manager's virtual box to a virtual position, combine the four attributes of a virtual position at your manager's level:

1) Responsibilities

2) Visibility

3) Resources

4) Reward

Now is the time to force yourself to step into the virtual position we just constructed. You must understand and subscribe to the priorities at that level, as well as to reason and make decisions at that level. Compare your virtual decisions with real decisions from your manager, calibrate your virtual position. The closer your decision is to your manager's, the closer your understanding is to that level. In general, the higher the virtual position, the more strategic your thinking should be. You are looking at much bigger issues with broader impacts.

Practice Multi-dimensional Thinking

Confine your actions within your real position; free your thinking at your virtual position. This is the best exercise to train your multi-dimensional thinking. The key to success when doing this exercise is to not confuse your real position with your virtual position.

Use of the virtual position will set your thinking free. The common mistake is to confuse the virtual position with the real position. Starting to give directions at the virtual position will get you into trouble with the people who are guarding their positions carefully.

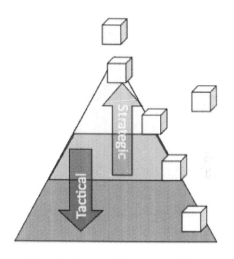

Elevate Your Virtual Positions

You can never promote your real position yourself. But you sure can certainly "promote" your virtual position any time you want in your mind.

Just think at that level, provide suggestions and solutions, but never give orders and directions at that level. Remember, it is a virtual position. This is for practice only, it is for you to broaden your view and deepen your understanding of the next levels.

Build a Virtual Database with Questions and Use Cases

Step into an equal level virtual position when you are discussing business issues with your managers. It will be difficult at first because you really do not know how to talk or react at that level. Start the dialog with questions such as:

1. What are our organizational goals?

2. What are our top priorities?

3. What is the biggest problem you have?

4. What kind of support do your peers need?

5. What is your manager's biggest problem?

6. What are your CEO and other executive's pet projects?

7. Who is the executive sponsor for our current projects?

8. What technology interests our CEO and executives?

9. What is our vision and strategy regarding products, services and marketing?

10. Do you need me to coordinate any group event?

11. How can I help?

Another way to help you elevate your thinking is to read biographies and stories about successful leaders and companies. These books can help you understand issues at different levels and how successful leaders take on challenges. Books such as: *Good to Great* by Jim Collins, *iCon Steve Jobs: The Greatest Second Act in the History of Business* by Jeffery Young and *Sam Walton: Made In America* by Sam Walton and John Huey. Take a look at our suggested reading list in the Appendix at the back of the book.

Observing successful leaders within your reach can help you even more. Write down what you observe and internalize the principles and sound business practices while your memory is still fresh. While reading about and observing others, you can store useful stories and experiences in your successful virtual experience database for later use.

Identify key skill sets at different levels; invest

your time and money continuously to fill skill gaps. Skills are your tools; your mindset determines the outcome.

Out of the Box 3-D Solutions

Your virtual position will be different from the real position no matter how hard you try to copy that position. You will come up with different solutions from your various virtual positions. The magic of these virtual positions happens when you can truly deploy yourself into these virtual environments; analyze issues, pros and cons of solutions from an angle that is not yours.

The magic of the virtual positions happens when you are out of your own box and jump into others wholeheartedly. By looking at the same issue from three virtual positions, you are able to come up with a 3-D solution, solving three parties' problems. Your solution will be the super glue bringing the team together. The super glue producer is the leader of the group and will most likely be the candidate for the next promotion.

Walk Out of the SMALL YOU

You can never truly get into a higher virtual position if you cannot completely walk out of your small box; just like you can never fill the cup if you did not empty it first. Walking out of your own small box means you have to modify, if not completely give up, your own priorities and personal interests. Replace them with group priorities and interests. Be more excited about group/company success than your own personal success. Let your integrity be your compass and let business needs be the driver for your daily operations.

Sharing information is as important as sharing success, especially well-educated information and opinions. People around you will treat you as the center of information, solutions and source of able help.

Trade Credit for Trust

In the business world, trust is worth more than credit. Helping others and making them successful without claiming credit are the best ways to earn it. The trust from your team, peers and bosses is the most valuable asset you can possess and trust is the key to many future opportunities. You should never get angry that your manager presented your report on behalf of his team; instead, you should be delighted that he valued your input and work.

Convert "I" to "we" in your vocabulary when you talk about success. Recognize people who contributed to the success of a project profusely, in public. A thank you note or email goes a long way in promoting group success and boosting collaboration across organizations. A thank you note will reach a few levels above which also makes you a visible leader a few levels up.

Start a personal log of your accomplishments and the help provided by others and a second log with the same information for your team. These lists will help you with:

- Performance reviews
- Bragging list for yourself and your team
- Resume for your next internal and external jobs

A Google doc would be a good way to store daily or weekly logs. An organization should have a weekly dashboard that clearly demonstrates activities, issues and accomplishments. Weekly status is the way to brag about your team's accomplishment as well as your own. View this as communicating good news.

"Should I list the help I provided to other organizations at my annual self-review?" Absolutely! As long as you put in true effort and the result is substantial, you should absolutely list your help to other organizations as well as your leadership and solutions as your accomplishments.

Glass/Bamboo Ceiling

Many people asked us, "Is there a glass/bamboo ceiling?" Our answer has always been: It is up to you!

I still remembered vividly, just like it happened yesterday, I was five years old sitting on my father's lap. My late father was an English professor and dean of the college. He raised me in a micro western culture even though I grew up in China. We had piles of English books stacked up to the ceiling. He said: "You can do anything a boy does, but a boy cannot do one thing that you can do - you can wear pretty dresses."

I did many interesting things with my father; we planted vegetables, hatched chicks using light bulbs, constructed a chicken house, read western books and looked at stars in summer nights. That is why I chose Space Physics as my major for my B.S. and Environmental Science as my major for my M.S. I always studied these topics with boys and never felt a ceiling above my head.

Let us do an experiment. Put a big piece of board one inch above your head for a few minutes. Remove it. How do you feel when the board is removed? Pretend it is there 24x7 above you; you cannot jump or even raise your hands without bumping into it. Yes, your growth will slow down because of its existence.

When you lift that invisible board off your head, the sky is the only limit! Remember the world is full of opportunities and true business leaders are trying to find real talent regardless your gender or nationality.

Refuse to accept this as an excuse for not getting ahead in life. You are the owner of your own career. It is up to you!

Get rid of excuses! No one should be a victim to a ceiling, imagined or real. It is illegal to discriminate in the workplace. If there is really discrimination in your organization, find a new job.

Three Bodies of Knowledge

It has been at least seven years since I last met Wade in person. Seven years of time washed away many grains of sand between us and left only sparkling gold.

I could not help thank Wade for one of my most important career paradigm shifts. Without his advice, I could not grow from a first line manager to a director. Wade looked at me with his signature smile, "Let me tell you my version of the story." My heart was racing; did I remember our meeting totally different?

Wade was an architect at a large software company 20 years ago. He once talked to a Sr. VP and his mentor at this large company.

His mentor said:

"Wade, there are three bodies of knowledge for each person:

1. The knowledge you are aware of, and you know it very well and apply it in your life daily.

2. The knowledge that you are aware of, but you don't know it well because you have no interest, desire or capability to acquire it.

3. The knowledge that you are not aware of, you never knew such knowledge existed. You will go through an important career breakthrough when you become aware of such knowledge and start to learn and apply it to your daily life."

Newly found knowledge liberates your thinking and provides you with a new frame of reference. You will enter a new paradigm where you will find new interpretations about relationships and events based on this new frame of reference.

The journey to maturity is to discover the 3rd body of knowledge continuously. We are expert in the first body of the knowledge. We make conscientious decisions not to pursue the 2nd body of knowledge when we become aware of our interests and limitations. We have to be secure and open-minded to uncover the 3rd body of knowledge.

Being secure and open-minded is easy to say but not easy to do. At the beginning of our career, we desperately try to prove ourselves to our senior leaders. We lose opportunities to have a paradigm shift conversation like the one between Wade and his Sr. VP.

The next time when you have an opportunity, listen and learn instead of trying to sell yourself to the senior leaders in your organization. Practice your newly found knowledge and you will be led to a new path that takes your breath away.

You Are Too Serious

John came to me at noon time. He opened our meeting with serious business topics talking professionally about projects and resources. After our discussion, he relaxed and smiled at me: "Elizabeth, would you please give me some feedback?"

I smiled back at John, "I would like to pass on feedback I once received from one of my mentors."

Harry, the Executive Chairman I worked for, had a productive meeting about software global resource strategy with me. At end of the meeting, I asked for his feedback. Harry looked at me with a serious face, "Elizabeth, you are too serious, and you are too scary!" Then he laughed.

What an astonishing remark! I was too serious and too scary! I viewed myself as a nice, flexible and resourceful professional. I knew for a fact that I was not outwardly humorous. However, I was not boring either! What could I do to correct that impression?

Solutions appeared. A few days later, my husband came home with a tip on effective communication with executives. He picked this up from his SVP, Mark, at a manager's meeting at Cisco. Mark required answers to these three questions at all his meetings:

1) What are you trying to tell me?

2) What do you want me to do?

3) How do you want me to feel?

Question number three never crossed my mind. I assumed that executives are super beings, with superior business acumen and judgment. I never assumed that their feelings were in the equation!

When we brief senior executives with facts and problems, we set the stage for solutions, prepare the senior executive to make decisions and let him know what you wish him to do.

However, seldom do we consider how we want our executives to feel.

We forget executives hold stressful jobs and they hear problems with and without solutions constantly throughout the day. They are people too. They have feelings and their feelings influence their decisions. We sometimes pass on our amplified stress at the end of a long day without thinking explicitly about how they will feel.

Once I started treating executives as human beings, respecting their time and feelings while providing suggested solutions with problems presented, I was no longer that super goal-oriented, laser-focused, scary and deadly serious person.

Now, when I talk to my teams, I asked the same three questions. Especially the 3rd one, how do you want your team to feel?

That is not Enough

My friend Suzy's New Year party has been the one that everyone looks forward to each year, not only for the great food, but also for gathering friends hard to meet. The party turns to magic and we laugh for hours. Suzy is a great businessperson, mom, wife and friend. We chat about life and our careers at her party. Suzy finds much wisdom among her friends and shares it with all of us. She recently visited a successful businesswoman in her late 70s. The lady shared the secret of her success:

"A person thinks he is very capable, that's not enough. People around them must think he is capable. Well, that's not enough. His manager has to think he is capable, however, that is not enough either. His manager must be capable. Even though his manager is capable, it is not enough. He must have great health. Without health and energy, it is not enough to be successful."

The take away from Suzy's party is: Exercise for great health, work hard, demonstrate your skills and strengths, follow a great leader and you will be successful.

Winners Compete with Themselves

I have been asked many times about competing with others. New graduates have asked me how to compete with experienced professionals; experienced professionals have asked how to compete with offshore cheap resources. These questions came from fear of the unknown.

My answer has been, "Don't compete with others; compete with yourself." I believe that every individual is a star, made of strengths and weaknesses. If you try to compete with thousands of people equipped with thousands of different strengths, you put yourself into a meaningless panic mode, chasing someone else's tail every second. If a company is chasing every competitor, it puts itself in the same situation and loses its direction. You can only have one brand effectively.

Let us fly up to 1000 feet and take a five-year look forward at you and your competitors. Identify your strengths and weaknesses. Pick one or two areas, which you would like to improve. Then compete whole-heartedly in these limited areas.

Winners never compete with others; they compete

with themselves. They set and calibrate their strategic goals and work hard on meeting these challenging goals. They stay focused on their goals and never allow competition in the marketplace to sidetrack them from their direction.

How to Manage Up

Managing up is about managing expectations from the corner offices and providing visibility and information to your managers, keeping everyone updated with your and your team's latest accomplishments, risks and solutions. You are also your manager's internal marketing agent to get all the good news out and spin the best news into challenges. You are his external marketing representative to get speaking engagements, award nominations and take advantage of board member or advisor opportunities.

Managing up helps your manager to be more successful and keeps him informed with the right amount of information, the thrill from risk and solution combo and bragging rights for the organization, on a weekly basis. Communication is the name of the game!

My friend Jason's boss told him, "No surprises for me. If you do have a surprise for me, I want to know the solution at the same time."

Managing expectations requires providing background information ahead of time, constructing the right frame for your projects. Answer the question before it is asked. Executives are fully aware of risks, challenges and headaches; they are supportive in providing resources and flexibility in scope or timelines. They trust your best intention and effort in driving the project forward. They are grateful you are part of their team.

The right amount of information and visibility for senior leaders and teams is critical. You can achieve this by using a color coded project status dashboard; weekly briefing status reports that contains links to detailed information that is only one click away or copying your boss FYI on critical events. The rule of thumb is that each piece of information should take less than 5 minutes to consume.

Risk and solutions are highly entertaining. It is your best opportunity to shine. Risk attracts attention throughout the organization; the person with clever win-win solutions is the hero who saves the day. Be the hero and give out credit and bragging rights to your boss.

Is it good enough to become your managers' best personal friend? Not really. It helps to play tennis or golf with your managers to build emotional bonds, but the bond may not be business-oriented enough to keep you from being fired for some mishap. He might help you to find another job after firing you from his team.

However if you use these buddy activities to conduct parallel communications, provide insight, information, risk and solutions to your manager, you can turn the emotional personal bond into a strong business-oriented bond. Moreover, that can become a serious mentoring relationship that goes beyond a job or two.

How to Deal with an Insecure Manager

Over the last 7 years, hundreds of people asked me how to deal with insecure bosses. Some of my audiences want to change their insecure managers. They share instances and behaviors of their insecure managers. Some cases are pretty severe:

One manager checked every line of code his employees wrote. He worked 7 days a week, 12 hours a day to check on every detail from everyone.

Another manager never allowed his employees to talk to anyone outside of his own team, no email exchange, no meetings with other teams without him being present.

Then there was the manager who took his team's inventions and filed patents in his own name. He would not let his employees lead any initiative.

The worst manager I heard about spied on his

people, watching over their shoulders to find out what each employee was doing. He was defensive and openly humiliated his people, putting his team down.

Can you change your insecure managers? No one can change anyone. They can only change the way they view or treat others.

Insecure managers often are defensive because of their low self-esteem and lack of trust. They do not trust either themselves or their employees. They demand absolute respect from their people, something that can only be earned not demanded, and order people around like crazy. They discard people's valuable feedback and attack people whenever they feel threatened. Team culture and morale are down the drain. There is not much you can learn from them, it is not fun to work for such a manager.

A people hire A+ people, B people hire C or D levels of people. When your manager is insecure, he is probably a B, or below, player. This type of manager will never build an A team; you will not have the opportunity to work with a super talented, motivated team. Synergy and collaboration are absent. So move on if your 2nd line manager has no plan to replace the insecure manager.

Homework

1. Construct higher-level boxes for

- Your manager
- Your manager's manager
- CEO
- VP of the business unit

2. Define key skills and quality

- Leadership
- Understanding of the business
- Communication skills
- Ability to attract talent and build strong teams

3. Put yourself in the box with everyday issues around you

- Make your virtual decisions
- Compare with the decisions from the real person
- Find out the differences
- Calibrate your virtual positions

3

Setting your Goals

When I talked about goal setting, many people shook their heads, "It is too hard to define goals, because the world is changing all the time. Any goal could be outdated in a month or two. Therefore, there is no need to discuss or define my goals."

True, our world is changing continuously, but not everything is changing. There are constants we can count on besides the sun, moon and earth. Long-term career and family goals are stable enough to be written down and measured periodically for their feasibility and effectiveness, almost the same as a company's vision, strategy and quarterly goals.

I changed my major several times from Space Physics (B.S.), to Environmental Science (M.S.), then Atmospheric Science/Satellite Remote

Sensing (Ph.D.) to Computer Science (M.S.). I am an executive who is an expert in organization management, software development and leadership coaching. Was my career an array of accidental events, drifting from one major to another major, one position to another randomly? Was there anything that did not change at all?

Most of us have burning desires throughout our lives. These desires change, on and off, clear and foggy from time to time. One thing that did not change much for me was my desire to learn, love and live to my fullest potential.

The Burning Desire

When your burning desires strike, you are sleepless for countless long nights. When you witness some greatness from another human being who just accomplished something extraordinary, or someone or something worth your unconditional love suddenly appears in front of your eyes, your eyes water, heart beats faster and blood churns like ocean waves. Your frame of reference is no longer the same.

Your burning desires provide energy and keep you more optimistic toward setbacks. They force you to meet challenges and overcome obstacles. They push you to fight worthwhile battles that affect your career and life goals.

What if that never happened to you? What if your logical mind and routine or mundane life filtered out any emotional waves and prevented you from discovering your deepest burning desire, your deepest unsatisfied spots in your heart? How can you lift that logical filter that clouds your heart, uncover your burning desire and let it be the light-house for your journey?

Let us begin the discovery process with the end in mind, by discovering our life goals.

Lifelong Goals - Vision of your Life

Lifelong goals are the clear vision about who you want to become. Your vision can only be limited by your energy and imagination. It is different from your burning desires. Burning desires will change when the scenery changes along your journey. It dominates your short-term goals. Lifelong goals change slowly, in most situations, lifelong goals stem from childhood dreams, distilled life experiences and lessons. Sometimes life goals contain philosophical greatness and grandness. I call my lifelong goals the "4Ls":

1) To live to my fullest potential

2) To love the people around me

3) To learn and mentor every day

4) To leave a legacy – help others reach their fullest potential

Some people would comment, "What a set of lofty goals of life. They are not practical enough to live a real life!"

Lifelong goals can be:

- Practical

- Specific monetary targets

- A set of career achievements

- Social status

- Impact on the world

Examples are:

- Earn financial freedom ($5 million savings/$10k per month cash flow)

- Start a company before age forty

- Have three accomplished children

- Become the president of the United States

- Discover the best way to produce green energy

- Get promoted to a Director position in five years

- Get promoted to a VP position in eight years

- Get an MBA in two years

- Be the head of a professional association in three years

- Buy a 3000 square foot house in your dream town

- Own ten rental houses in twenty years

- Retire at age 50

Goals could also be character enhancement goals instead of social status, positions and financial targets. Many of us make character enhancement a lifelong continuing process, which makes us more polished and sophisticated people. Music, literature and many other activities bring more satisfaction and enjoyment to our lives and relieve stress. Fulfilling these goals makes us a more complete human being and allows us to resist more severe life crisis, enables us to withstand many less fortunate life events and helps us to build stronger character.

Among these practical goals, which is the one to provide you with the most emotional satisfaction that you will do whatever it takes to realize? That is the one that captures your burning desire.

Three Levels of Lifelong Goals

The reality starts from the quest for your burning desires and goals at higher levels. Your life is the result of daily decisions and choices made based on your goals.

You can never get what you cannot see or do not know. You can never create things that you cannot envision. Life is accidental if there is no goal. Our life goals either liberate or limit our potential, experience and accomplishments.

Lifelong goals reflect three levels of mindsets (3 S):

- Survival
- Success
- Significance

Many people set their goals too low, only at the survival level:

- Pay off mortgage
- Save money for children's college fund
- Survive layoffs

They save every penny to survive downturns. They work harder, take more abuse from work, take pay cuts for more workload, but will all of these help their survival? Temporarily they will help survival, but will hardly make them winners in the long run.

If you are searching for answers to become more successful, then you are looking for possibilities and risks you can take to get there. You will discover winning strategies.

Significant goals can elevate us from our own interests to group and community interests. These goals integrate individuals to a higher cause and larger group. Bigger accomplishments and impacts can possibly be achieved. When a person's goals are significant, he can draw a tremendous amount of positive energy and talent around him. This person naturally constructs win-win deals and relationships with others. A win-win person wins and so do people around him. However, a successful person might gain his success at the expense of others, therefore, these successes can be temporary.

If you are longing for significance, you sometimes have to sacrifice a normal personal life; you strive for greatness with your physical and emotional energy.

Leaving a Legacy

When I first came to the United States, I was very lucky to know Pat and Lou. They helped me tremendously during my first few years here.

Lou was an extraordinary man; he was in his 80s when I met him in the early 1990s. Lou had taught at Ohio State University, he also served in the US Army Air Corps during World War II and the US Air Force during the Korean and Vietnam Wars. He gained the rank of Colonel before retirement. Lou was a great engineer and a successful businessman. He devoted time and energy to mentoring and helping others throughout his life.

I asked Lou one day, "Why do you spend so much time helping me and other people you have never met before?" Lou smiled back, "I help you because I believe that you can be more successful with my help. I will not live that long to see your success, but it will become my legacy whether I see it or not." Indeed, he did not live long enough to see all the successes from the people he helped, but I certainly add my successes to his legacy.

Many people, like Lou, help others unconditionally. I would like to share a poem written by a teacher, Shirley Yates, who lived her life fully and happily through her 90s. At her request, her family printed this beautiful poem for her funeral:

Legacy

When I die, give what's left to children,

If you need to cry, cry for others walking beside you

Put your arm around anyone,

Give them what you need to give me.

I want to leave you with something,

Something better than words and sounds,

Look for me in the people I have known and loved

If you cannot live without me,

Let me live on in your eyes,

Your mind and your acts of kindness

The body dies and love does not

So, when all what's left is love, please give me away!

We all received a lot from people like Lou and Shirley Let us thank them. They helped us build our success, let us help them build their everlasting legacy.

Feasible/Realizable Goals

Burning desires will burn you out if there are no solid incremental and short term goals in place. Lifelong goals will become lifelong dreams if you glide your life through without solid short, medium and long term goals. All short-term goals are stepping stones for you to reach to your highest life goal and satisfy your burning desires.

To help our students identify their goals, we always asked them to write down:

- Lifelong goals
- Burning desires
- 20 year goals
- 15 year goals
- 10 year goals
- 5 year goals
- 3 year goals
- 2 year goals
- 1 year goals
- 6 month goals
- 3 month goals
- 1 month goals

Each goal is the staircase that supports you to reach the next level, altering goals at any level will alter your destiny. Measuring each goal also validates the path you designed for yourself.

What Makes you Happy

Happiness is a goal for many people. Some people feel happy when they have money in the bank, accomplished children, a nice retirement house and good health.

Pat is happy when she feels needed and she is accomplishing something that is good for others. She has volunteered throughout her life. After her retirement at age 44, she has committed to volunteering helping adults learn to read, write and speak English. She likes people, they give her energy. She enjoys baking and sharing her goodies with others.

I am happy to share my career experience with other professionals. I am excited when I teach classes and speak at conferences, encouraging people to develop a mentoring network.

I also love to grow roses and share these beautiful flowers with school teachers, office mates and neighbors. My fresh organic vegetables are pretty popular at my office. Sharing tasty, healthy food and beautiful flowers brings a lot of joy to my life and others.

These activities are the engines of happiness. Spend time on the activities that create happiness and you will be happier regardless of whether you have achieved your other goals or not.

Goal Discovery Questions

Personal goal discovery questions:

1.   What is your burning desire?

2.   What is your biggest pain point?

3.   In 1, 5, 20 years and end of your life

-Where do you want to live?

-What position do you want to hold?

- What kind of social status do you want to have?

-What kind of family do you want to have?

-What kind of friends and social network do you want to have?

-How much money and other assets do you want to have?

-What kind of skills do you want to acquire?

-What kind of reputation/personal brand do you want to have?

Go through each question, write down detailed goals, and pair each goal with your emotional satisfaction when you achieve them.

Consider group goals:

• What is the official and unofficial company mission?

- What group goal was in your last year's review?

- What kind of problems kept your managers up at night?

- What do the company leaders talk about repeatedly?

- What is the biggest problem/pain point in the team, your 2nd line manager's team and at the company's level?

Validate your understanding with your manager or trusted advisor at your company.

Hire the Company When It Hires you

Pat suggested to me to hire the company when it hires me. When you are interviewed by a company for a job, you need to assess the company and the people who interview you and ask the following questions:

- Is this the right match for you and your talents?

- Do you want to work with these people?

- Do you like the company's values and culture?

- Do you believe in the company vision?

One recruiter said, "You must look two jobs up from the job you are taking. You need to define what lessons you will learn from the job, who will teach you these lessons and what valuable experience you can gain from this job. You should also define the graduation time from this job, the time when you should have learned enough from your job and are ready for the next challenge."

You may not leave the company when you graduate from your current job, you may apply for new positions and acquire more responsibilities from your current organization.

Skills for the Next 24 Months

Based on your long-term goals and your current job requirements, you can easily find the set of missing skills that prevent you from qualifying for the next job.

Assuming you want to become a first line manager in 24 months, find a job description of a first line manager at your company and ask your manager, mentor or HR partner to identify your skill gaps. In most cases, an individual contributor would have the following skill gaps:

1) Presentation skills

2) Project management skills

3) Business understanding

4) People management skills

5) Cross functional collaboration capability

If you can construct a virtual box for your next job, you can practice from that box daily and sharpen your skills when you have the opportunity.

Align your Goals with your Company Goals

You might be very lucky that your personal goals are totally in line with your group goals and company goals. However, we all run into challenging situations that are beyond our control, especially in building your careers when your personal goals are not coupling well with your surroundings, the company, team, manager and customers. Here is the question, "Should I surrender my own goals for the good of the company? Should I escape from my limiting surroundings or are there other ways to handle the situation?"

It depends.

If your goals conflict with your company's goals in principle and integrity, find a new company without detrimental conflicts. Be very selective and even use discriminating criteria.

If your goals are in line with your company's medium and long-term goals, but not short-term goals, find the group within your company that supports your short-term goals. When your personal goals are fully in line, you have the best chance to reach your full potential and contribute the most value to your company.

If you buy into your company's goals at all levels, decide to surf along the wave, calibrate and shift your short-term goals, take the ride!

I have seen very skillful and creative professionals who are able to create their own position within an organization. They re-defined their jobs, wrote their own job descriptions and contributed a unique value to the organization. If you do have the vision, opportunity and ability to sell it to upper management, write your own ticket!

I have also met a lot of extremely hardworking professionals who did not have a clue about their company, group goals or understanding their organizations' values. They were puzzled by their stalled career and under-valued contributions. The question I asked was, "How do you even know if you are contributing to the most needed area, to the most critical mission of the company without clear and deep understanding of your company's goals?"

They replied, "How do I know my company goals?"

The answers lay in your company annual reports, all-hands meeting presentations and your staff meetings. Answers can be found from chatting in the elevator or at lunch table discussions with your manager and other senior management team members.

"How do I relate these high-level superficial goals to my job?" Ask your manager. If you are not satisfied with the answer, discuss goals with your trusted advisers/mentors/experts, your manager's manager or peers. Validate your interpretation with your manager.

When you are showered with multiple tasks, ask yourself, "Which one can make a difference with my group goal?" Make that task a higher priority and verify this with your manager.

When you talk to leaders at different levels within your company, make sure that you practice your virtual positions in Chapter Two. Practicing grants you the freedom to be in and out of these positions easily, to step into virtual positions to internalize the meaning of the organizational goals and priorities.

The truth is, your daily tasks must relate to your company goals and group goals to make any difference; otherwise, you should leave that job and find a new one which makes a difference.

Validate your Goals

Having a list of feasible goals and checking off the goals when you accomplished them is very satisfying. We need to make sure that our big goals are made of smaller goals that are achievable. The satisfaction from the achievement can refuel our engine and keep us moving forward.

Sometimes, we set ourselves up for failure. When your goals are too grand or too remote from reality, break them into small puzzle pieces; acquire them when you see opportunities. Review your goals regularly to make sure you can accomplish them.

Homework

1. Write down:

- Your company and group goals

- Your burning desires

- Your lifelong goals

- Your 1, 2, 5, 10 and 20 year goals

2. Align personal and group goals:

- Validate your goals with your group goals and company's goals

- Calibrate your goals regularly with reality, either slow down or accelerate your goals.

4

Branding

The word branding came from the practice of burning a letter or logo on the hide of an animal with a hot iron to declare ownership. The concept advanced to general product recognition, such as Dove soap, Coca Cola, Nike, and every product in the marketplace. The term has evolved into professional branding to distinguish oneself from others. Every professional needs a distinct brand, just like every product in the marketplace. A distinguished brand can trigger a relationship or event formed without your physical presence. Such a relationship or event can be a job inquiry, business partnership, expertise consultation and even promotion candidacy.

What is a Professional Brand - An Open Book

A professional brand is about who you were, who you are and more importantly who you will become.

It contains your past, your present and your future. It also contains your knowledge, experience, potential and more importantly your vision about who you are and who you will become. A personal brand is like a living and ever-evolving book which has its name, front cover, back cover, preface, table of contents, acknowledgements, references and chapters of rich content.

The Name of the Book - Who you Are and Who you Will Become in Less Than Seven Words

The name of the brand is what you call yourself, what represents your passion, your future and your accomplishments in seven words or less. The name of your brand is unique; it represents the person you want the world to recognize. The name is the most distilled version of your personal vision that translates into the person you will become in the future. The name of the book has the most distilled version of your brand. For example:

- Thomas Jones, successful entertainer

- Steve Jobs, extreme re-inventor and excellency builder

- Elizabeth Xu, leadership coach, senior engineering executive

- Pat Zimmerman, mentor and community contributor

Front Cover - your Image Perceived by the External World

The front cover is your image to the external world; the image you designed purposefully or obtained accidentally. The front cover is on display 24/7; there is no way to hide it. There is no way to alter it overnight.

The front cover can be very logical, vivid, colorful or simply just graceful or powerful. It can be just black ink on white paper; it represents the contents of the book. No matter what kind of cover you display, people around you from various distances can see a different you, from different angles, in different lighting, backgrounds and time. The impressions on your front cover are the reality of other people, regardless of your intention. It is ironic that no matter how crafty you are, your external image is often different from the one you crafted. Just like "beauty is in the eye of the beholder," images are supported by opinions, interpreted and stored in different minds. The reality is that your external image is the reflection of your own projection and other people's perception. Be prepared to accept it and continuously calibrate and renew your image.

What is your Front Cover

Your front cover consists of the following impressions you obtain through your daily activities:

- Look - your clothes, hairstyle, makeup, jewelry and health
- Talk
- Smile and other facial expressions
- Body language
- Interaction with others
- Stories you tell others
- Quotes you believe in
- Gadgets you carry
- Car you drive
- Computer you use
- Family pictures on your desk at the office
- Your professional network
- LinkedIn profile and recommendations
- Blog
- Papers and articles published
- Speeches given

Think about someone you know, the first image that appears in your mind is that person's front cover to you. Each person has a spectrum of his front covers which exist in his social and professional circles. If you collect and analyze a person's front covers, you can predict his next two years of career trajectory.

The composition of a professional image:

Past	Present	Future	Career Trajectory
80%	20%	0%	No potential
20%	60%	20%	Grounded with high potential
0%	20%	80%	Dreamer disconnected with reality and little potential

Many retired people who have not discovered a new hobby and only live in the past, constantly talk about their past with no regard for the present or future. Many young college students only dream about what is in the future, but ignore the present. They do not utilize their experiences and their knowledge to secure their future opportunities.

A manager who wants to have rapid career development should consider a virtual position two levels up from where he is, even dressing like people one or two levels above his job grade. He wants to master the skill of thinking two levels up and possess the ability to communicate two levels up. In this case, he should be able to look, think, speak and act like the role to which he is aspiring.

LinkedIn is your Public Front Cover

Several years ago, Bob, a Sr. Manager updated his LinkedIn profile with a director title before he got his promotion. His VP called him in and asked him the reason. He said that he was on the way to director and his team was big enough so he should get a promotion very soon. The VP asked him, "What kind of impression do you want to create for your network? Do you want people to trust you or not? Do you want people to discount your integrity?" Bob thought about it and decided to take his inflated title down.

Once I interviewed a very good candidate who had relevant experience for a key leadership position. He listed his position at a company as a VP on his resume, but on his LinkedIn, the same job was a contractor job. The position discrepancy caused us to question the candidate's integrity. We decided not to offer him the leadership position.

I strongly recommend you update your LinkedIn profile and make sure your resume is in-sync with your public profile on LinkedIn.

Back Cover - Our Images Perceived by Friends and Family

The back cover is the image you show to your family and friends. When you are on display your back cover supports and keeps you grounded.

Some of us have relatively plain back covers in comparison with our front cover. There is no need to dress up and be on display with your relatives and friends. You can be yourself.

Some of us have consistent front and back covers, our personal life is equally, if not more, colorful than our professional life. We usually have a richer network and social life.

Our back cover is constantly filled with unconditional love or other emotions. Flaws on the back cover sometimes get ignored by our family and loved ones.

What is your Back Cover

You show your friends your personal image throughout your personal life and interaction with them:

- Your circle of close friends
- Your social activities
- The style of your house, furniture and garden
- The books on your shelf
- The music you play at a party
- Social engagements
- Charities or organizations you support

- Your cooking style

- Recent vacations

- Your hobbies

- Sports and exercise

- Facebook profile and activities

Preface - your Motivation and Passion

We are all animals with motivation and passion. You might have more or less passion or perhaps you have not uncovered yours yet. Spend a week or two thinking about your motivation and passion, then answer the following questions:

- What is your vision about your life, professionally and personally?

- What are your goals?

- What makes you happy?

- What do you most appreciate and love?

Table of Contents - the Index of your Rich Experience, Skills and Knowledge

Let us assume that you are very accomplished, but your accomplishments are not known by others. What is the best way to show others your greatest accomplishments, experiences and knowledge? How can you make this information available for the whole world 24/7? What should you do to present this information to others who are searching for talent? The answer is: make it search-ready!

How to Make your Greatness Available to Search Engines

An open book to the public is necessary to get yourself known in the industry and world. The best way is to index these great things and make the index ready to be searched. Three effective ways to index yourself for others to search are:

- Online resume

- LinkedIn detailed profile

- Bio at your own website or blog in multiple languages, if appropriate

How to Write an Effective Resume

Writing an effective resume has never been an easy task. You can find a long list of books about writing an excellent resume and numerous blogs about writing resumes. We would like to share some helpful tips with you:

- Limit your resume to 1-2 pages

- List your most recent job duties and accomplishments first

- Talk about numbers of people you

supervise, money saved, money you control

• Emphasize your education, internship, and/or volunteer work if you are a new graduate

• Use strong action words, e.g., driving instead of manage, establish instead of start, designed instead of helped, led the team instead of participated in a team

• Make your resume searchable: many resumes are fed through a computer, or given to a non-technical clerk. Both the computer and clerks only look for key words.

• Embed technical terms into your resume in the qualification summary

• Customize your resume using the same terms from the advertised job descriptions

• Write one resume per job application instead of one resume fits all

Google yourself to see what your prospective employer will see if he googles you.

You can perform the following online tests:

1. Google your name, count how many correct hits on the first 5 pages, each correct hit is 1 point

2. Search LinkedIn for a person with your

credentials. If your name appears on the first page, add 10 points, 2nd page, add 5 points, 3rd page, add 1 point

3. Go to YouTube to search yourself, to see how many professional related entries come up, each video counts 5 points

4. Google the topic where you consider yourself an expert, see how many hits about you are on the first two pages, each hit is worth 2 points

Bonus:

1. Google your name, find out how many hits are on the first page. Each hit is 1 point

2. If you have a blog: +5 points, every blog published in last 12 months, add a point for each.

3. If you are on LinkedIn with a picture: +5 points, each recommendation is 2 points.

Add them all together:

Congratulations if your score is above 50! You are visible! You have a viable online presence.

Below 50, you need to work harder.

Above 100, you have a great online presence.

How to Write an Effective LinkedIn Profile

A LinkedIn profile is your online resume and your online professional face. It opens opportunities for you. People have asked me how I got my SVP jobs. It was from LinkedIn! Recruiters searched my LinkedIn profile, recruited me to two SVP jobs and requested numerous VP/SVP/CTO/CEO level interviews, sometimes several interview requests within a month.

If you browse through 60 connections in your LinkedIn, 20 in your level, 20 one level up and 10 two levels up, 10 at CEO, CFO, CTO, CMO, SVP levels. You will notice the difference. CMO and VP of Marketing/Sales usually have the most professional and effective online profiles. Here a few helpful tips:

- A professional looking picture is a must!

Dress in professional attire, headshot only. No dogs, evening dress, swimming suits please. Light makeup and jewelry, limited Photoshop modification.

- 3-5 recommendations, 1-2 recommendations from each job

- A tag line, one sentence about who you are and what you want to become

- A summary paragraph about your skills and expertise, including key words and acronyms, this paragraph is for search engines and recruiters

Chapters - your Rich Experience, Skills and Knowledge, in Detail

Think back about your life, everyone goes through phases, ups and downs intellectually, emotionally and physically. Everyone goes through dramatic or slow flow of normal events in our personal life and professional career. These events may include:

- School

- College/degrees

- First job

- New jobs

- Moving to a new place

- Getting married/divorced

- New babies

- Promotions

- Layoffs

- Departure of good friends and family members

Most people learn from these events and gain a tremendous amount of knowledge, skill and experience. Internalize these events and distill them into insights and wisdom. When someone passes away, we all wish that they might have left a book of their life, but it is too late. When we tried to remember what we did 50 years ago, the smell, excitement, colors, movement, lights, passionate conversation will fade just like everything else.

When you go to an interview, you may face the following questions:

- What is the most challenging project you participated in/drove/managed?
- What are your best accomplishments? What could you do better to double the results?
- What is your biggest mistake/failure? What did you learn from that experience and what would you do differently next time?
- Tell me about a project/product you designed and implemented.
- Tell me about your hobbies.
- Tell me about the most exciting news you have heard.
- Tell me about your best managers and worst managers.

Will you have time to think and find the best answer to these questions on the spot? Not at all if you want to ace the interview and get your dream job. Plan how you will answer these questions before everything fades away.

Try writing out about 10+ stories about your-self (so you will have these stories in your head.) Each story should be less than one page long, so you can talk about it in 2 minutes. These stories will be the baseline for your answers during tough interview questions, or they allow you to make conversation with strangers or colleagues more interesting. The purpose of this exercise is not to memorize your answers, but address questions in advance so you are ready with a reasonable answer when you are asked the question. Do this so you are not fumbling for a reply. You may even tape your answers so they sound natural. You do not want to memorize answers, just use your own words.

How to Write "Chapters" - One Page Stories

The nine attributes of each story can be:

1. Name of the story - the purpose
2. When
3. Where
4. What
5. Skills and experience gained
6. Challenges
7. Lessons learned
8. Distilled insight and wisdom

9. What if: what would you change and what would be the outcome

The story is about you, others are just parts and characters in the event, to assist you to reach the outcome. Tape your story and time yourself, limit your story to 2 minutes. You may lose your audience if your story is longer than 2 minutes.

Branding is an Ongoing Effort

If you know exactly what your brand will be, that is great! Your vision about your life will drive the design.

Find a person you know well who has a similar brand. Review their LinkedIn summary and tag line and get their advice on how to build such an external image. Also find a few people you would like to become in 5, 10 and 20 years, learn some distinct attributes you admire for your brand in progress.

Each milestone is a trigger point to remodel your existing brand. Feedback from your professional network is invaluable in the architecture design phase before you start to tear down your LinkedIn page or completely rewrite your resume.

Creating a unique brand can be done in a few days. It requires you to understand yourself inside and out, your life vision as well as career goal. You must be willing to do things that make you stand out from the crowd.

After the brand is created, you need to raise your brand, just like you raise your kids. This is a daily activity that is part of your professional life, it never stops. Once you have decided on your brand, you cannot continually change it left and right. This causes confusion to those around you.

Your brand changes over the time. Pat successfully built and launched her career several times after her retirement from AT&T at age 44. She became an outstanding literacy tutor. She was recognized nationally with the Jefferson and Kennedy awards for her outstanding contribution as a community volunteer She taught and grew senior college in Reno (Osher Lifelong Learning Institute at the University of Nevada, Reno), into a 1000 student senior college. Now she has become an author and teaches at Stanford with me.

It is never too late to create your unique brand, tend it carefully, feed it daily and raise your brand through K-12 and college, you will have a suc-cessful brand that accelerates and enhances your career.

Homework

Build your brand:

1. Get your professional picture taken.

My picture was taken by my son when he was 10 years old. The secret is to take 50+ pictures using a professional digital camera. It is best to use natural light and stand in front of a light colored wall. The best time to take the picture is before 10 AM or after 4 PM inside a bright house.

Dress professionally and be sure to represent your image correctly. You should look professional, energetic and friendly. Are you willing to put this picture on your LinkedIn, blog site, email profile, company websites, conference websites and your business card?

2. Review your life vision and career goals.

Your vision of life_____

Your career goal_____

Who you are_____

Who you want to be in 2 years _____

Remember that your vision drives your goals and your near-term goals. Who you want to be should be reflected in your brand.

3. List five things that you did that makes you

stand out from the crowd. Write 5 stories 2 minutes each, time them.

1.

2.

3.

4.

5.

Your five standout accomplishments and endeavors might not be winning Jefferson and Kennedy awards. You are not alone! Select five things that align with your professional goals. If I wanted to build my fashion brand, the fashion I designed and made in the 80s would be a great item on this list, but not the team leadership award I won at IBM.

Follow the 9 attributes to write relevant stories.

4. Build a professional LinkedIn profile:

- Picture
- Brand name
- Summary of your qualities
- Specialty

- Job history

- 3+ Recommendations

Every month or so, update your network with your new accomplishments, travel information and conferences you attend, new books and articles you have read.

My favorite LinkedIn profile is from Mark Hill (http://www.linkedin.com/in/markrhill), a VP of marketing when we worked together. I would like to suggest you reference his well-written LinkedIn profile.

5. Print your business cards:

- Name

- Brand name

- Picture

- Blog link

- Vision of your life (optional)

5

Prepare for your Opportunities

You get a 1000-piece puzzle for your birthday, however, these pieces do not come with a picture of the final assembled puzzle, can you get it assembled?

You probably say, "There is no way."

Over our lifetime, we get more than 1000 opportunities. Can we use these opportunities to build a meaningful life and career? Can we recognize and capture these opportunities?

Luck is Prepared Opportunity

Many successful people say luck is on their side. One test was conducted when the ABC 20/20 TV program placed $20 bills along a half mile long street. People who always said they had good luck found most of the $20 bills; people who never felt they were lucky hardly found any in the same setting. Unlucky people simply do not look for their opportunities, or do not recognize their opportunities. Therefore, they usually miss the chance to realize unseen opportunities.

In the year 2000, many Silicon Valley engineers made millions of dollars on paper from their unexercised stock options and unsold stocks. Only a very small percentage of them cashed out. Most had only seen the stock market rise; few had experienced a recession or even worse a depression. Few of them considered that life could be different from what they were living if they cashed their paper money in at that time. They never considered this as a once in a life-time opportunity to be financially independent. They held on waiting for their paper money to grow. Most of these paper millionaires missed the opportunity to cash in their options, becoming real millionaires and earning financial freedom. When they went through the job market down-turn in late 2008, they wished they had cashed out their unexercised freedom.

Ten plus years later, most of these paper mil-lionaires have less net worth than in 2000. If we cannot recognize career opportunities presented to us today, ten years from now, we might be in the same position as the paper millionaires, or even out of a job.

Why Can you not See Opportunities

Opportunities are presented every day. However, not everyone recognizes these opportunities; therefore, they cannot make use of them. Consider these situations:

- Some people have no clear goals to connect to opportunities. They are super drifters who drift with random ocean currents.

- Some have no clear understanding what skills and experiences are required for the next level. Their career goals are not well understood and defined into feasible steps.

- Some people are not willing to commit extraordinary effort to use the opportunity to build extra skills and experiences required by the next level positions.

- Some people are not willing to take the risks that come with opportunity; they see more risks than opportunities. Risk scares people from utilizing opportunities.

People without clear goals drift with the current, chase bubbles or slide with downturns. They are reactive, but seldom proactive. Many of them become very good at reacting to whatever happens in the world. They are flexible and quick to survey the situation. They are very proud of their drifting ability. Their careers become water molecules inside of a microwave oven, oscillating back and forth lightning fast, generating heat and spikes. How exciting! Unfortunately, these heat spikes are random energy conversion. Their energies are not channeled in a well-defined direction. These heat spikes are not going in a focused direction like laser beams, therefore, their energy dissipates without making any visible imprint on their career.

Some unlucky people do not think they deserve some awesome opportunities because they are scared of the responsibilities and risks associated with these opportunities. Opportunity and risk are best friends, they always come in pairs. A risk-taking attitude allows you to lift the cover and discover the real value of that awesome opportunity.

Lucky people (and I believe people make their own luck) who have goals and continuously calibrate their goals, always look for the next few stepping-stones leading to their next milestone. Opportunities come in masks/costumes, colors and forms that you would not expect. Opportunities present themselves under different lighting and at different speeds. A pair of well-trained eyes in front of well-defined career milestones can x-ray these opportunities and compute their true value.

The courage to take a risk and the thrilling results from that opportunity, urges you to raise your hand and open your heart to that awesome opportunity. Life itself hands us many opportunities. We live through the thrill of ups and downs, getting satisfaction from self-improvement and reaching meaningful goals.

The Puzzle of Life

The first puzzle I bought for my son was a 10 piece Winnie the Poo puzzle. We played with it together so many times I could put the pieces together with my eyes closed. Puzzles became more complex as my sons grew older. When we opened a 1000 piece puzzle, looking at 1000 small pieces in similar colors and shapes, we wondered whether we could ever put them together. Fortunately, every puzzle came with a finished picture on the box. With that in mind, we were able to put the right pieces together and complete a puzzle in a reasonably short period of time.

Life is like a puzzle, it hardly presents you with the finished product. We often run into thousands of puzzle pieces (opportunities). Without a big picture in mind, we cannot look for pieces that can contribute to that big picture. Our long term goal is the big picture, our mid and short term goals are the detailed designs in that picture.

Every career milestone consists of skills, positions and timing. We can certainly break it into puzzle pieces, and collect these pieces along the way.

Life does not present us with a big finished picture.

We should create that big picture and design its details. We need to recognize and grab opportunities that contribute to that big picture continuously.

Accelerate your Advancement

The game of life resembles a video game. In a video game, you collect different kinds of points and treasures along the way. Good positions and timing accelerate your point accumulation. Once you make enough points, you can leap forward to the next level.

When you cruise through the game without knowing the rules and how to achieve bonus points, you can never collect enough points within the permitted time to enable you to go to the next level. Therefore, never wait until you are fully ready to take the next level job. Take a risk to earn bonus points and accelerate your advancement!

Six Essential Leadership Skills

There are six categories of skills that make or break a leader:

1. Strategic Formulation

2. Customer Orientation

3. Business Strategy Implementation

4. Being a Team Player

5. Leadership

6. Personal Traits

Understanding these skills will help you to recognize your opportunities.

Strategic Formulation

Current and future leaders must be fully immersed in the industry direction and new market developments. In the technical industry, the leader must be able to either act as a technical visionary or be able to work well with technical visionaries, learning essential technical content quickly to formulate competitive strategy. In a non-technical industry, a leader must know what kind of new technology is available and how this technology can improve his company's competitive advantage.

This leader must also be able to provide sound analytical insight to improve his company's competitive position and increase competitive advantage.

This leader must be able to simplify the situation and have the ability to get to the heart of complex issues quickly. He must be able to explain complex issues in such a way that everyone on the team understands him.

The most important skill in strategic formulation is multi-dimensional thinking. The ability to jump from abstract levels of thoughts to the operational level with feasible implementation steps and back to abstract level of thoughts and theories again. This ability allows the leader to continuously refine processes and adjust directions according to reality and stay focused on the most important direction in execution. The leader who masters this skill can handle complexity and uncertainty by observing situations from different angles.

Multi-dimensional thinking also enables the leader to achieve a broad and balanced perspective through the ability to see things from other people's virtual boxes. He can quickly come up with a win-win solution among his peers, customers, employees and investors. Our Virtual Box Model in Chapter 2 is an effective tool to enhance multi-dimensional thinking skills.

Customer Orientation

When we talk about business, we actually talk about satisfying our customers' needs and monetizing customer satisfaction. The more satisfied our customers are, the more competitive and differentiated we become in the market place.

Some leaders want to sell their services to customers without listening to customers' needs. Leaders should proactively understand customers' specifications with regard to:

- Services

- Reliability

- Maintainability

- Usefulness

They will drive the team to exceed these expectations. Staying competitive, continuously offering new services and reaping new market opportunities keep a business vital.

Customer needs are seeds to our innovations. Leaders should not just implement what customers are asking for; they should channel customers' needs to their new products and offerings. The ability to understand customer needs, utilize technology and services to channel customers to innovative services and products puts the business among market leaders.

When iPhone woos the market by its superior usability and elegance, product usability becomes the market trend. Leaders who only interpret usability as beauty is only skin deep, try to win customers with beautiful colors and slick layout without looking into what unique services need to be provided to satisfy customer needs. Amazon's

Premier Membership is nothing slick or colorful on its website, but it wins millions of repeat customers. It provides unparalleled user experience that requires negotiations with shipping services, suppliers and flawless execution in 2-day free shipping. True usability is beyond a beautiful website and product interface.

Business Strategy Implementation

Leaders should be decisive. I have observed leaders who asked so many questions for such trivial issues, that they slowed down execution speed and sucked a risk-taking spirit right out of the organization. When leaders are indecisive, market opportunities are lost and costs increase.

Leaders should move quickly and objectively to gather information and resolve conflicts or restructure ventures. They understand when and how to use various decision-making skills including using authority, consultation and consensus. They make quick tough decisions including terminating poor performers. Making quick decisions with limited data and in an uncertain situation is discussed later in this chapter.

Leaders should focus on continuous improvements. They should encourage continuous learning about the market, technology, management skills, organization structure, process and execution of best practices throughout their organization.

Leaders should be experts in effectively using structure and control systems. They design both permanent and temporary structures to optimize the use of human and material resources and accomplish business objectives faster and at lower costs. They drive organizations with priorities and manage dependencies and exceptions. This allows teams to keep their autonomy and efficiency. These priorities provide guidance for team collaboration in uncertain and ambiguous situations.

Ability to influence is the most advanced skill for leaders. Even if you are the CEO of the company, you still have to master this skill to influence your board, shareholders and customers. Steve Jobs is a good example of using his personal charisma, passion and product vision to influence his board, shareholders, customers and his troops.

The fact is there are very few Steve Jobs who are able to influence the world in such an extraordinary fashion. Ordinary leaders have to work with key stakeholders inside and outside their companies, get ownership or buy-in from these important stakeholders, keep them informed and turn them into a network of resources and supporters. They also need to engage with customers and keep customers informed about emerging product developments.

Being a Team Player

Being a team player is a big challenge to a leader's ego. Leaders should work with their colleagues to create an egoless environment where corporate-wide goals drive decision-making across organizational boundaries. Occasionally, they have to sacrifice the interests of their division or department in order to support corporate-wide goals.

Another challenge is to proactively listen to different points of view and build rapport with people who are different from the leader himself. Leaders can form effective alliances with different people in the organization and achieve congruent goals for the corporation. Building virtual boxes for your alliances can help you understand them and form win-win solutions.

Leadership

You are recognized as a successful leader of the organization when you can inspire people and channel their collective efforts to accomplish a common vision. Leaders should be able to build trust within their own organizations. They involve their team to set goals together, and gain buy-in during the goal setting process. Buy-in is a must, you cannot expect a team to accept a goal and give their all to achieve it just because the boss set it as a company goal. The team must see the value and agree to make it happen.

Leaders should have the ability to inspire their team:

- Clearly state what results are possible to achieve

- Clearly communicate to the team what each member must contribute in order to provide superior values to customers

- Understand employees and be able to enlist them by appealing to their values, interests, hopes and dreams

Leaders should clearly state organization values through multiple communication channels and through their own actions. Their actions speak for them more effectively than their verbal and written communication. That's talking the talk and walking the walk.

They develop people by providing timely coaching, opportunity, visibility and recognition. Measuring and rewarding outstanding results can change team behavior more effectively than criticizing or ignoring wrong behaviors.

Personal Traits

Leaders should accurately assess their own abilities. They should know their strengths and weaknesses. They should proactively measure self-effectiveness and adopt best practices. They need to be fast learners and proactive listeners. They should be fair and consistent to themselves and people around them.

Leaders also should have strong self-discipline; they need to persist in working out problems and discover win-win solutions. Their perseverance helps them to overcome resistance and obstacles, succeeding even in situations which may appear to be beyond their control.

Leaders should have energy to manage at the executive level. They can maintain high performance under constant high stress. They have the ability to get the job done and execute the committed plan without delays. That means identifying the most important issues quickly and applying the resources to get issues resolved, shortening critical paths continuously, to effectively utilize resources and maximize opportunities.

Where to Find Opportunities

Opportunities are everywhere, but very few will go to your cube on their own if you do not have a distinct well-known professional brand. You need to search for them:

- Help your peers with their projects

- Volunteer for jobs within and outside your company

- Participate in networking events

- Contribute to your professional network

- Publish expert opinions

- Blog and participate in professional forums

- Setup job search agents

- List your resume on job sites

- Stay on top of new technology and trends, position yourself as the leader of new ideas and technology

A distinctive and well-known professional brand includes a trustworthy reputation and a well-connected professional network, two essential factors to attract more opportunities. Reference Chapter Four to build an effective brand and Chapter Eight to build an effective professional network.

Paths between A and B

The path from career position A to B can be random instead of linear; there are many combinations. You can collect different puzzle pieces at different times and speeds if you follow different paths. Do not look at the world as black and white. There are millions of colors in the reflected light even from a tiny dewdrop. There are different paths to achieve the same goal as well. Spend some time thinking through possible combinations. When one of the possible combinations appears, grab it. Everything happens naturally if you think ahead of time and raise your hand to claim it in a split second.

Opportunities are Puzzle Pieces Between Positions A and B

Standout from the Crowd

The world is full of talent and you are one of them. Many people stress out just thinking about the fact that the world is producing more talent each day. Standing out from the crowd is not easy. Your professional look, excellent presentation skills and commanding presence help you to stand out. However, these skills are not enough to help you stand out in all situations.

When senior executives look for talent, they look for the new leaders who have a bigger heart and broader views, which can look after the company's interests and collaborate with others to understand and drive business needs.

Moreover, senior executives look for talent who can communicate with them at a similar level.

They are also looking for the leader who can communicate goals and strategies to their teams clearly; who can simplify complex business situations and identify key actions to achieve significant results.

Furthermore, senior executives also look for leaders who can attract and guide people who are smarter than themselves and build productive and creative teams.

Finally, the candidate's positive attitude, confidence and passion toward that opportunity will seal the deal.

Be Part of your Company's Succession Plan

One of my former bosses asked me, "What do you want to become when you grow up?" I joked back, "I want to become you!" He looked at me seriously, "Are you sure?" I replied seriously, "Yes, and would you please mentor me?"

My boss was a very seasoned and secure leader, he mentored me tremendously. Later on, he told me, "I saw great potential in you, but never knew what you wanted and how much you wanted it. I did not want to waste my time on someone who did not want to reach their full potential." I still get helpful career tips from him, even from his Happy New Year email.

If your boss is a secure leader, present your potential first, then let him know you want to be part of the succession plan when opportunity arrives. People come and go in the business world. All wise and secure leaders love to have multiple succession plans throughout their organizations. In a well-run business, if one person quits, the successor can step in within 48 hours. A secure leader never leaves an organization without a successor.

If your manager is insecure, talking about a succession plan with him is a suicidal career move.

Humble Leaders are Never Alone on the Journey

You are not alone to face the challenges if you are willing to learn. You will need help and guidance from your managers after you get the opportunity. It is part of their job to help and guide you. Your team will support you to solve problems. All this guidance, help and support will be there for you if you are humble enough to ask for it and are confident enough to engage others from Day One.

Failure is OK

Opportunities come with risks; and some risks do bring failure. It is not our choice to avoid all failure. However, it is our choice to either learn from failure or let it defeat you.

Some people like to become victims, putting themselves in a pity pot, and blaming all failures on others. Unfortunately, they never climb out of their cozy pity pot.

Some like to beat themselves to death for their failures. These past failures kill their spirit and courage. They do not believe they can be successful the second time around, so they run away from future opportunities.

When you fail, look into the root causes of these failures. Are they caused by:

1. Things beyond your control and influence

2. Things beyond your control but under your influence

3. Things under your direct control

Ignore things that are beyond your influence. Focus on what you should have done differently to change the outcome. Look at the gaps from your strategy, skill and execution capability, as well as missing supporters, advisers and mentors.

There are many contributing factors beyond your control, but they can be under your direct or indirect influence. If you are given a second chance, would you engage and influence people differently, earlier or have more involvement with them? Remember, things that are beyond your control may be under your supporter's control.

The best you can learn from failure is to expand your knowledge and confidence. You also can find more creative ways to handle challenges, mitigate risks and influence things that are beyond your control.

Why Improve English Skills

Many of our readers are immigrants or first-generation Americans and need to improve their English language skills. Why? Actually, you can live your entire life in the United States without speaking, reading or writing English, if you live in the right place. There are Chinese, Korean, Japanese, and Spanish doctors, dentists, bankers and grocers in pockets around the country where these immigrants live. People have many reasons for not improving their English: I do not have time to work on my English; I am busy working and raising a family; my children will learn good English skills in school. You are fooling yourself if you tell yourself these things. You really will never get ahead in this country or the business world without reading and writing English fairly well.

Learning the language of the country where you live broadens your world, opens up opportunities, gives you freedom, helps you gain general acceptance of others and makes your children proud of you.

By learning the language, you widen your world. You can enjoy movies, television shows, plays, lectures and read English newspapers, magazines and books. You learn and can participate in what is happening around you. You can go to your child's school and actually speak with the teacher. You can help your child become a better student. You can read contracts so you know what you are signing, as well as signs for directions and safety. You can become an independent person.

Language opens up opportunities in the business world too. You can participate in group discussions, give presentations and take an active role on a team. If you just sit through meetings without offering any suggestions or ideas of your own, the others in the group may think you are not too bright and have nothing to offer. Usually you have a lot to offer, but are just too afraid or shy to open your mouth and express an opinion for fear others will not understand your words. If you leave all those wonderful ideas in your head, unspoken, is it any different than not having an idea?

If you want to build your business, products, or offer special services, you need to understand the culture and product-use patterns in the marketplace. Without proper English skills, you will have a hard time building sophisticated products and services for your business. Do not worry about having an accent. The United States is a very large country. Each region has its own accent so sometimes Americans have to listen hard to understand Americans from other parts of the country. This country also likes to think of itself as the melting pot of the world. People from all over the world come to work and live in America.

Most immigrants do not lose their accents unless they learn the language before they are eleven years old. Accents are okay as long as people can understand what you say. In fact, I think they are charming.

Knowing the language is liberating. You can communicate with doctors, dentists, bankers, grocery clerks and waiters. You can actually give a clerk the correct change to pay a bill and do not have to be fumbling for change or pay with large bills and hope you are getting the correct change in return. You can participate fully in business situations, not sitting on the sidelines afraid to speak.

You gain general acceptance of others when you are can understand what is being said and act appropriately. You can respond to everyday questions: What color would you like? May I see your driver's license? How many would you like? What size do you take?

Make your children proud. Your children should not be your translators. You are the parent. Most likely one of the reasons you came to this country was for a better life for you and your children. That is admirable. You gave up a lot to travel thousands of miles to a different culture. Embrace this culture and learn the language for yourself as well as your children. You deserve to have a good life too. You deserve to do something good for yourself. You deserve to take some time to improve Your life.

Often you can find English as a Second Language (ESL) classes conducted by volunteer organizations that are associated with international organizations such as Pro-Literacy America or state organizations such as Cal Lit. Churches, libraries and community colleges offer English classes and tutoring. Classes are offered at all times of the day and night so they are convenient for the students. Some groups offer classes free of charge while others charge a fee. Look around and find the group that best fits your needs. Update your skills and become a part of this country we all call home.

Pat is a volunteer tutor who has been teaching adult literacy and ESL since 1989; she has taught several thousand people since then. Pat not only teaches language, she also teaches American culture and values. She inspires me to contribute back to the community, take many risks and pursue a professional career in industry.

Build Business Vocabulary

The first challenge I encountered was acronyms and business jargon when I joined IBM Santa Teresa Lab (STL) in 1996. Most businesses use such jargon; sometimes different departments within the same company use different abbreviations and terms. Think of it as a specialized business shorthand. Technical designs were full of acronyms as if they were written in a different language. My technical lead John printed 15 pages of acronyms and definitions. I tried to memorize them, which was a Mission Impossible task. I gave up after several tries during my first month at STL.

Not knowing these acronyms was a terrifying experience. I could not understand the topic being discussed in group meetings. I was an outsider. I did not know what was being said.

I made up my mind after three months of embarrassment that I would learn and use these acronyms as much as I could. Six months later, I found myself inventing new acronyms and using them in my technical docs and meeting discussions.

When I took a new job in the insurance industry in 2010, I started with an education class and learned acronyms as fast as I could. All new hires in my organization were given the acronyms and on-line recorded presentations about the insurance industry. We significantly shortened new-hire on-board training time. I also discovered that immigrants were not the only new-hires needing this class. Most people hired from outside the industry needed it too. It was a business shorthand for that company.

When new technology is invented, a list of new business and technical vocabularies are invented too. Some of the existing terms are overloaded with new meanings. A new trend of technical discussion becomes technology fashion. The same kind of trends are in management and leadership discussions, just like in the clothing and music industries.

We are living in an ever-changing world, learning or refreshing a few business words every day is a part our life whether English is our first language or not.

English is a living language, constantly changing and adding new words. Words that started out as texting abbreviations have now actually made their way into our dictionaries.

Decisions vs. Choices

We make decisions and choices each day, sometimes leisurely, sometimes forced. Each decision or choice points to a different path, defines our future and influences people around us, subtly or profoundly.

Similar to programming language, life presents us with sets after sets of *if else* statements. We could very well come from the same place in our lives (e.g. classmates from the same school). Each outcome of the *if else* sets us apart. Over a long period of time, we become vastly different people. Therefore, some of us become restless when it is time to make decisions, others are afraid of the consequences of their choices.

I had an enlightening conversation with one industry technical leader. He was the first person ever who clearly separated decisions and choices for me. He said, "Choices are made based on pure facts, based on adequate supportive information; it is a purely analytical result. Decisions are made based on partial facts, partial experience and a lot of intuition and intellect. Making a decision without adequate facts requires judgment and leadership." He applies his theory at work where he trains his team to choose well and to make conscious decisions.

His theory explains why many people have a hard time making choices or decisions. Ironically when enough facts present the obvious choice, emotional factors frequently jump in and polarize that very obvious choice. On the other hand, when information is limited, principle, guts and intuition should and must rise to drive the decision. Often people opt to look for facts which might take a long time to obtain or even be impossible to get. This situation imposes a huge cost on opportunities. Using his principle, leaders must know when to decide and when to choose, and then the rest is easy.

During my sons' ski break in 2011, Lake Tahoe was buried in snow. We stayed inside for two days. Were we bored? Not at all. We looked forward to the evening Jeopardy show between Watson (the IBM analytical software running on IBM super computers) and the two best human Jeopardy champions. My 9 and 12 year-old sons talked about Watson all day long. They guessed who would win and bet on the outcome. As you may know, Watson, defeated the two best human Jeopardy champions, a major milestone of computer analytics and artificial intelligence advancement.

Watson reminded me of my early years (1996-2000) at IBM. It brought back memories of my trips to the Watson Research Lab. We worked days and nights and delivered the first commercialized Digital Watermark, Cryptolope (encrypted envelope for secure content delivery) and Video Charger (video streaming over Internet) products. These products were many years too advanced to gain massive market adoption. Watson also reminded me of the analytical engine and Business Operation Intelligent product my teams built at Vitria in 2007, which helped business professionals understand the meaning of an ocean of data, search for patterns and boil down to a few pieces of relevant data to help them gain insights and make better, quicker choices and decisions.

If you watched the Jeopardy show, you may have noticed that Watson made choices based on facts and data. When its data did not present a dominate choice, he skipped that question. Yes, Watson could not make decisions when data was not sufficient. Watson could not raise meaningful questions on its own; it could choose questions from the list on the screen. Watson is indeed a computer; Watson is a piece of advanced analytical software, Watson can only make choices but not decisions.

My young boys were not ready to accept the defeat. They argued and decided that humans have the advantage of curiosity, creativity, intuition and passion over machines. I could not agree more. When a group of the right people get together, sparks of creativity and synergy can help them go far beyond an array of machines. Sparks would destroy any super computers! My sons cheered on our way back home with relief, because they suddenly realized that Watson was created by humans. The two best champions were defeated by a group of scientists who are excellent in building an analytical engine and acquiring relevant data from the human knowledge base to make better and faster choices.

Leaders make decisions when there are no obvious choices. Real life business is not as straight forward and factual as Jeopardy questions. Our intuition, creativity, passion and courage to take risks enable us to make quick decisions in a timely manner. Moreover, real life business does not have an option to skip a question. You have to make decisions one way or another. The ability to make that sound decision will make you stand out as an obvious leader when people are confused by inadequate data.

Making Quick Decisions with Limited Data

During my talk at Microsoft in 2009, a program manager shared her frustration on having trouble making quick decisions with very limited data, say 10-20% of data. Her manager considers this ability as one of the major indicators of professional maturity. I agree with her manager. But how can one make quick decisions with very limited data?

The key is to become systematic in the decision making process. Summarize and build decision-making models that take a few parameters. If you construct many simulation models in the business world, you can change a few parameters and provide quick conclusions. Once these models become part of your thought process and intuition; you can accelerate your decision-making process significantly. Of course, you can always compare with incoming data and validate your conclusions again.

Observe the senior people around you as they face the same challenges. Find out how they come up with quick decisions and why they think the way they do. You will be able to learn and construct your models very quickly.

Understanding the precision of the decision and conclusion is also very important. In this fast changing world, you are expected to give an educated guess with 60-80% accuracy instead of 99.9% of accuracy. It is simply okay to take a guess or give a quick conclusion. When you do that, add a disclaimer of your precision along with your conclusion. When AT&T was a complete monopoly, they would develop a product and then test it for a year or two. At divestiture when tele-communications became open to any business who wished to participate, AT&T had to change the way they did business. Their mantra became, "Do it, fix it, do it." It meant, make the product and offer it to the public as quickly as possible. If something is wrong, fix it and put it back on the market. They no longer had the luxury of testing, testing, testing products for long periods of time.

Homework

1.   Identify the next two major milestones you wish to try to achieve

2.   Identify possible opportunities in your company.

3.   List all puzzle pieces (skills, experiences, projects).

4.   Assess your skills.

5.   Identify the top three skills you need to improve in next 6-12 months.

6

Planning for Action

Goals without opportunity are just wishful thinking. Opportunities are random puzzle pieces for people who have no goals. When we connect goals with opportunity, it is possible for them to become reality.

Once you found and captured the opportunity for your goals, you have the chance to try them out. How are you going to utilize your newly obtained opportunities effectively?

Action without an execution plan is a recipe for disaster. A carefully designed action plan will set you on the path for success.

How do you write recipes for success before you take your first step?

Career Master Plan

At the beginning of your career, a plan can be as simple as written action items and timelines as a check list. Modify your plan as you are working on it. However, when you are in senior management and executive positions, you have to have a sophisticated master plan which consists of multiple levels of specific sub-plans. These sub-plans are integrated and supportive of each other to achieve maximum returns. You have to treat every opportunity as a start-up and run it as a real business. A career master plan is the key to your successful career. It may consist of:

- Clearly defined missions and goals

- Clearly defined professional brand

- Alignment with the company or the industry big picture

- Acquiring partners and advisers

- Internal and external marketing plans

- Acquiring support at all levels within your company

- Developing and refining solid execution plans in your daily business operation

- Career risk analysis and mitigation

- Staging the change to push your plan forward

- Skill and resource validation with reality

- Feasibility and easy implementation check

- Progress check regularly

- Rewarding system for yourself and others

Your plan may consist of other elements that are unique for your own situations. For example, if you are an immigrant, you might want to have a plan to learn the local culture and language, which will help you understand local business and easily generate synergy with your colleagues.

Your career plan should also be part of your overall life plan such as your family life, your children's education, your financial plan, your lifestyle and retirement plans. Your vacation plans should be there too to avoid burnout. Vacation plans can be part of your children's education plan. Travel is mind expanding at any age.

Clearly Defined Missions and Goals

Clearly defined missions and goals prevent you from getting lost or side tracked. Sometimes people drift during the execution phase; they forget their mission and real purpose, start to work on secondary priorities or something that is interesting but counter to their original goals. They shoot themselves in foot and fail at the last minute.

As a business leader, the first question you ask yourself in the morning is, "What am I going to do to direct my team to the most important task toward our mission?" The last question in the evening is, "Did my team and I work on the most important task toward our mission? If not, what should we do differently tomorrow?" The same set of questions should be asked about your own career each day too.

Stick with your mission and goals, adjust your plan to allow you to accomplish them with fewer resources and limited time. That is what a good leader does.

Alignment with the Big Picture

Every company has finite resources and time to compete with other companies. You have to utilize your resources wisely and maximize the Return on Investment (ROI) for your company.

How can you make sure that your plan is strategic to your company? Most companies list its top priorities during board meeting presentations and at all hands meetings. Public companies present their top initiatives at quarterly shareholder meetings. If your projects are not mentioned at the company all hands meetings for the last 12 months, your project may well be not that strategic.

What should you do if this happens?

Change to lead the most strategic projects or lead the worst area that needs a strong leader. Either direction represents fast changes. The faster changes are, the more career growth opportunities they bring to you.

I personally welcome a turnaround situation that the only direction you can go is up if you can identify and fix the root cause of issues. Most likely, you will get resources and support from your company to move forward with your plan to turn around the areas that are performing the worst.

During the 2008 economic downturn, most companies needed to reduce the bottom line and increase the top line. A new project can be strategic if it addresses either or both lines. In the ever-changing market, new products and services will emerge constantly from competitors and new customer needs. It is also possible to propose and lead a new initiative and strategic project. If that happens, you successfully align your career plan to your company's big picture.

Acquiring Partners and Advisers

The 21st century is no longer a *super hero* century. The global scope of business and the explosive amount of information are well beyond one person's time and energy to digest and come up with intelligent decisions. Your best partners can be a Human Resources (HR) partner who will be your perfect sounding board and personnel management advisor, your peers in Marketing, customer support and sales who will provide customer insight and marketing trends, or Engineering who will save you in tough technical challenges if you are in other departments. Your advisers could be your mentors, your bosses and board members, who have a view of the big picture and help you stay on the right track.

Keep your partners and advisers informed, not only for getting help, but also to provide them with business operational insight, which is critical to their job as well. Asking them if there is anything that you can help them with or risks they observe will make it a two-way business relationship. They will also feel more involved and get a lot of satisfaction from developing talent.

Developing and Refining a Solid Plan at all Levels

Some leaders have only one level of plan residing in their own head. The plan is only about them, not integrated with the company, organization or teams who support them. They keep their career plan so personal, that no one knows their game plan, no one knows how to support or guide them.

Since their career plans disconnect from the rest of the world, their plans also insulate themselves from a vast majority of business opportunities. There are not enough vehicles to carry out their career plans.

Building a plan is like building a house, there is no way to build the 10th floor without a solid foundation and nine other floors below. Once your career plans are integrated with the company's strategic projects, you are no longer working on a personal plan, you are working on the company's projects and you have a chance to get help from multiple levels. If this company project is successful, it certainly helps your personal career.

Reviewing a plan with multiple levels within your organization is also a buy-in and alignment process. You will be amazed how creative and talented your teams are, how knowledgeable your advisers are and you also have a chance to contribute to these plans and build on top of each other's to come up with better plans.

During these reviews, let your team know the real purpose of the project, the value to the company, customers and individual team members' career growth. Let them know the whole story, it will set their creativity free, become motivated and productive, and all of you will be on the same path to achieve your career goals.

Staging the Change

Living in this ever-changing world, any well-established methodology and process should be constantly re-evaluated and changes will be required to perform an outstanding job.

Changes are hard to implement when people are used to the old ways and not inspired to change. No one can ever change others. He can only change himself. You can motivate people to want to change, but only they can change themselves. Personal interests are strong motivation to inspire changes.

People are also motivated by their own ideas. Best leaders plant seeds in the minds of their team, prompting them to produce desirable ideas. Inspiring leaders are excellent in getting creativity going. People like to walk under the light from their own light bulbs. Best leaders let the team take the credit and lead the change themselves instead of pushing the team forward. The credit the leader gives out gains him more trust with the team, helps him plant seeds and lead more changes ahead.

Some leaders push change for the sake of change. They sometimes change processes and organization structures just to gain personal attention and stir up some activities without understanding the real reason behind existing processes and organization structures. Before the new leader gains the trust of the team, his changes and he himself become the target of failure.

At the beginning of my career, I wanted to become a change agent, pushing my own brilliant ideas and good practices. After a few bounce backs and bruises on my forehead, I learned that the best change agent stages changes and inspires others to change instead of changing everything himself. It is necessary to have the buy-in from your team to make a change successful.

When AT&T was going through a reorganization combining two departments into one, they created a program called Building on the Best to sell it to the employees, to get buy-in of the change. The idea was to take the best practices of each organization and use them in the new organization. People who created these best practices are your best allies, their outstanding results solve your problems and already demonstrate a path to success. Results speak for themselves and for the changes you want to implement.

When you stage your changes, classify the changes and introduce them with small and local changes based on bright spots (local successes). Socialize the concept of future excellency you want to instill, then gradually move to grand and fundamental changes. The second change should be introduced after you have secured and completed the first change, when your team fully embraces the concept and is inspired by the new direction. The team who adopts bright spots grants you the trust to move forward with future changes.

Again, building virtual boxes for the people you need to engage will help you understand them deeply and motivate them easily.

Acquiring Support at all Levels

Communicate the benefit of your project to all levels of the organization and motivate them to support you. People will support you if you consider their interests in your projects. In many cases, you have conflicting interests with some other departments. These issues should be addressed and resolved early to make the change go smoothly. Perhaps the other department has a better idea to implement the project, and there might be a win-win solution in the making. Conflicts should be dealt with early, so satisfactory outcomes can be agreed upon.

Your partners and advisers will also provide support for your project if you continuously engage them.

Resources, Skills and Tool Validation

Many new leaders ignore details and assume that all resources are equal and all resources will be there for them. The reality is, every resource is different, especially highly specialized senior resources. Every single resource already has multiple assignments, priorities and ownership. Rarely is everyone 100% available at the time you need them. Validate your plans with your resources and obtain their commitments before you start the project.

Tools are also important. Discover or build effective tools for your project, such as Wiki for information management and Microsoft (MS) Projects to build a solid plan and track all your work tasks and resources.

Green Slopes vs. Black Diamonds

If your plan does not work on paper, it will never work in reality. Check whether the current technology supports your plan. Also look for easy ways to implement and maintain the finished product. Is the end product easy to use? Does it fit the client's need? Will the scope of the project fit into the right time-frame for the market?

When we ski, we train ourselves hard to get on black diamonds, the hardest ski trails. We are proud to be on black diamonds. However, when we work on projects, we are looking for easy ways to accomplish them. We are looking for the green slopes, the easiest ski trails. Are there green slopes? Can I make it easier for the team? Can I steer my career toward the green slopes?

Plan Status Checks and Calibration

A leader is like the captain of the ship. Give your team your near term and long term priorities. At the same time, you have to constantly watch the direction and check the status of your ship to adjust your priorities. Auto pilot can work temporarily, but not permanently.

Designing a status report in a certain format that contains critical information for the team is important. Status is a two-way street. You should give the team updates on what is happening outside the project they are working on while they inform you of their status.

Planned calibration, based on the project status, will keep your project on track. Calibrating a project is another round of small scale buy-ins and updates. Clients and executive sponsors are facing dynamically changing business situations. A flexible implementation team will help them embrace changes and continuously stay successful. When they are successful, your project is successful. That sure helps your career.

Reward System

How to reward people should be considered at the very beginning, never an afterthought. Rewarding is a continuous activity. A timely reward is more important than a big reward. The best way to reward people is within 24 hours of the success: a note, an email, a pair of movie tickets, a gift certificate for coffee or a flower from your own garden. There are many ways to reward people who contribute and go beyond their normal duties.

Always reward people who help you. Sometimes the reward may be a promise of future help. Deliver your promises on time and be flexible in helping your partners who depend on you.

Innovation and Process

Many people would say I am a process junkie because of my extensive experience at IBM DB2, and many years of practicing sophisticated software development processes to build large scale mission critical enterprise software. The perception from people who do not know me well is their perfect reality. Indeed, I look like a process junkie on paper from afar.

People who know me well see a different Elizabeth, who has a passion for innovation. Research, innovation and creativity inspire me, and fuel me through many boring days and activities. Without innovation, one would never paint the most moving scenes and objects; one could never build killer apps. Without innovation, the iPhone would never have reached our palms.

Well, can we build an iPhone without any process? Despite the many birth defects the iPhone IV had when born, it went through very strict processes to achieve such consistency, friendly user interface and it is a piece of art.

When I go to an empty parking lot and zigzag whatever way I want, I can be as creative and I can drive as slow or fast as I wish. When a few more cars appear in the parking lot however, I have to be less creative in my driving pattern and follow the parking lot rules to avoid an accident. When I drive on Highway 101 along with others at 65 mph, I have to follow the traffic rules and speed limits. However, my mind can be as creative as I wish. My car can be decorated and equipped with creative colors and gadgets no matter where and when I drive.

When we are alone, facing an empty parking lot, a piece of fresh canvas, or a new MS file, let our imagination and creativity fly. When we are facing a half filled parking lot, a half filled canvas, or a half page essay, rules, theme, and consistency have to work with our creativity to complete our creative painting, touching essay or safe driving.

When we are on a high speed highway, when our peers are all working at 65 mph to construct sophisticated critical missions, rules and processes have to be there to ensure high speed parallel driving and avoid fatal crashes. Processes ensure that everyone can be as innovative as they can in their creative mind, the whole team can move at 65 mph without crashing into each other.

Processes can be innovation killers if the goal is all about orders and rules. Processes can stimulate team creativity and enhance team productivity when the goal is to build the most innovative products that solve customers' problems and they love to use. The key is whether the leader of the team knows how to fuel creativity and enforce rules and processes at the same time.

Life Planning

Personal plans should be considered as you develop your career plans. The first day you start your first job, you should consider your retirement plan and financial plans. We talked about setting your goals of life in Chapter 3, these goals can be realized only if you build a detailed and actionable plan behind it and schedule time and resources for each action.

When speaking to college students, I sense their life struggles, no matter if they are in the greatest universities or community colleges. Their concerns are almost the same: grades, jobs, social challenges, fast changing industries and job markets, financial difficulties and lack of confidence in their future.

I recently spoke to students from one of the best universities in the world, "You are living other people's greatest dreams! Everyone wants to get into this university." However, these students felt they were living in a nightmare and pressure came from all directions because there currently is no job market in the majors they love.

When I talk to high school students, their goals are simple - getting into the best universities. I can predict, shortly after they get into these great universities, they will face the same challenges as those expressed by other college students.

Someone asked me a few years ago, "Do you want

to be 20 years' old and go back to college again?" I thought about it for days and then decided, "No." I love the energy I had when I was 20 years' old. I would love to be young again, but I do not want to go through these struggles again. If you can bring your knowledge, experience and money back, do you want to be 20 years' old again? I say, "Absolutely!"

Thinking back, the biggest struggle I had was not having a sense of future, not knowing my life goals and not developing a life plan to avoid these struggles.

When I talk to college students, I sincerely share my goals and methodology to ease the pain from struggles. This has motivated Pat and I to write this book.

Homework

1.   Define your life plan.

2.   Define your career master plan with actions and dates behind them.

3.   Evaluate your career plan with company goals; define a change plan if your career plan does not fit into your company's goals.

4.   Calibrate your plans and get buy-ins continuously.

7

Execute your Plans

Vision without Execution is Hallucination

Thomas Edison once said: "Vision without execution is hallucination." I have met many young professionals who were passionate about changing the world and becoming outstanding business leaders, but failed repeatedly.

Many years ago, one ambitious team member stood in front of my desk, "Elizabeth, you cannot even imagine what kind of person I will become in a year!" I saw fire in his eyes and heard his trembling voice full of passion. "Show me!" I sat back in my chair and calmly looked at him. I believed his intention would be convincing once he showed me his execution results.

I had dinner with four mentees from MJAA. The food was good, the conversation was even better.

Brenden, one of the mentees, asked me, "What's the one thing that made your career successful?"

I replied without hesitation, "Execution."

What's execution? Execution is about systematically carrying out your plans and accomplishing goals and reaching milestones. The author of *Execution: The Discipline of Getting Things Done*, Larry Bossidy, defined it as, "In its most fundamental sense, execution is a systematic way of exposing reality and acting on it."

Execution is about using self-discipline tenaciously to examine the reality of your environment, your assumptions, goals and milestones. You are also taking accountability for your own career (never allowing yourself to fall into the pity pot.) Always find better ways to get things done and realize your career goals.

You are ready to execute now if you have internalized what has been suggested to you in the last six chapters. We helped you identify the purpose of your life, elevate your thinking, establish goals and plans and capture opportunities to realize your career goals. Let us assume you have done everything we suggested, you are ready to rock and roll!

Effective Execution

My student Katy asked me, "How do you get so much done when you have only 24 hours in a day?"

Excellent question! Sleeping less than 6 hours per day and working more than 60 hours every week is not the answer. Effective execution is about working on the most important tasks and producing the most impactful results (return) within the same amount of the time (investment). The higher the return over investment (ROI), the more effective your execution becomes.

The Time Jar

A well-known time management theory is called the Jar Theory. Assuming we all have the same size jar, which represents our time, we have four types of things to fill the jar:

- Rocks - the most important priorities of your life and career

- Pebbles - things you like to do, such as hobbies

- Sand - things you have to do, such as cooking and cleaning

- Water - things that are pervasive in taking up your time, such as watching TV

The Jar Theory: fill your jar with rocks first, put time and resources into the most important priorities in your life; then pebbles, fill as much as you can with things you enjoy doing; third, sand, fill the same jar with things you must do; and last, water, add things that are pervasive. If you fill your jar with sand and pebbles first, you will not have room to add your rocks.

One senior leader said he always scheduled his 10 most important tasks every month:

- 7 tasks were for his salary

- 2 tasks were for his bonus

- 1 task was for his good deeds for his organization, his colleagues and community

Once these tasks were on his schedule, he assured his time and resources to complete these 10 important tasks every month. These 10 tasks are the big rocks and pebbles he filled in his jar first, meetings and tactical tasks are sand and water to fill the rest of his jar.

Colorful pebbles will make your work and life more enjoyable and playful. As leaders, the ability to make work more playful just like a game can engage people and yourself. That creates synergy and establishes a unique culture.

Time Maps

If you complain that you are too busy and you have no time to work on strategic projects and learn new skills, you might want to look into where your time is spent each day.

Log your activities every hour for 7 days; categorize what you have done in the last 7 days into four categories:

- Rocks - the most important priorities of your life and career

- Pebbles - things you like to do, such as hobbies

- Sand - things you have to do, such as document your work and driving

- Water - Things that are pervasive in taking your time, such as watching TV, chatting with people

Plot your data into your calendar, color code your activities according to these four categories:

- Rocks - red

- Pebbles - green

- Sand - yellow

- Water - blue

Now look at your own energy zone. If you do have control of what you do each day, are you scheduling your most important tasks when you are the most energetic?

If you look at your time map, do you have enough rocks in your time map? Is there too much sand and water in your schedule?

An executive's time map is different from an engineer's time map. The executive has more strategic tasks in his schedule; he has to do a lot of heavy lifting each day. An engineer's day is full of normal tasks such as sand and water. Therefore your time map determines who you are and what you will become based on your schedule. Move more rocks into your daily schedule!

Cross Out Your Completed Tasks

Crossing out completed tasks from my to-do list is a most rewarding daily activity. Tools such as simple yellow stickies can improve your time management significantly. Once you unload the burden of remembering these tasks to a piece of paper, worries and stress are removed, you can focus on completing the task efficiently.

IBM provided employees with a "Things to do" pad in the mail rooms. I liked to use it every day. When I arrived at the office, the first thing I did was to write down what I wanted to do that day.

As the day went by, I crossed out completed tasks and added new tasks. Crossing out a completed task was extremely rewarding! I still have that habit today.

There are many new task tracking tools available; however, tools are only effective if we use them. Try a few and choose the one you can use every day, even just a simple blank piece of paper that you can write your tasks down on and cross out.

Multitasking and Parallel Projects

Multitasking is nothing new, we do that every day. We watch TV and read emails at the same time or talk on the phone when driving. I like to read email and write while exercising on an elliptical machine; I also like to wash clothes while I am cooking food. I feel particularly productive when I have all my machines going, washing machine, dryer and dishwasher. Somehow it gives me the incentive to continue working on other tasks.

Multitasking can be effective when you pick two or more tasks that demand different levels of attention. One task must be the dominant task on which you put 90% of your energy. Cooking requires more attention than washing clothes; reading email requires more attention than exercising; reading email requires more attention than watching TV. However, when two tasks require the same level of attention, we might not be able to do either very well, if we try doing them at the same time. Talking on the phone is equally demanding as driving. When we start to pay more attention to our conversation, we put our life in danger.

Activities utilizing different muscles can be good pairs of parallel tasks such as running and thinking, eating and watching TV (you might eat more when you watch TV!), reading and listening to music.

Multitasking at work can be dangerous too! If you are working on too many projects simultaneously, you might fail at all of them. Projects that require different paces and priorities are better parallel pairs than projects requiring the same pace and priorities.

Parallel Communication

Most of our communication in the business world is done on a one-to-one basis or through announcements in a conference setting. Consider using another effective way to communicate and get connected with your people, customers and business partners' - parallel communication.

Parallel communication means that you are talking to people while you are doing something else together. Lunch and dinner are good and commonly used parallel communication settings. While eating delicious food and drinking tasty wine, people are more relaxed and open to honest discussion. They tend to share more information than they do in a conference room setting. More personal alignments are discovered and people are more interested in doing business with each other. It is no wonder that many contracts are written and signed on cocktail napkins!

If you have difficulty talking with your teenage children, you might want to join them in cleaning their messy rooms without criticism. While working together, take this opportunity to chat with them. Ask about their friends, what they are doing in school; ask their opinions about the things happening around them. This will usually open up the communication channel between you. Hiking, playing games, dining, watching games and movies together are all good opportunities for parallel communication where you can strengthen the bond between you and your children and friends.

Team building activities at work are forms of parallel communication as well. People who can play together can work together. If you have just announced a difficult business decision and are worried about team morale, having a lunch with your key players is a good way to survey their issues and explain and share the reasons behind your company's difficult decision.

Effective communication is not only about what you say, it is also about how you say it and where you say it. Mixing tough topics in a more relaxed setting, while people's focus is on more pleasant and satisfying actions, can help your message penetrate faster. You can get real feedback from your team with little resistance.

Proactive vs. Defensive, Visibility vs. Excuses

My friend is an accomplished corporate lawyer. She constantly deals with big clients. Recently, she worked on a complex business negotiation with her company's largest client. The client was very skillful in applying various negotiation skills including changing positions, escalating and blaming her for delays, renegotiating terms back and forth.

She struggled through the long and unpleasant negotiation process. Finally, every party was satisfied and the deal was made. But she felt bruised inside and out.

When we went to lunch to celebrate the success, she asked what she could have done better given the same case again in the future. "What's the most troublesome issue you faced?" I asked my tired friend. She sighed, "Communications with the client, internal business partners and my boss were the hardest challenges I had. Everything became convoluted, the client's negotiation techniques mixed with their hidden agenda. I was accused of being on the defensive and making many excuses. Some information was true for a brief moment, and then became false because of ever-changing terms and conditions."

I was amazed. My friend is not the type to be defensive and full of excuses; she is humble and responsible.

"There are two pairs of conceptual paradoxes: proactive vs. defensive and visibility vs. excuses. Both can be used to describe the same action and same information, due to different timing", I said. "What do you mean?" she asked. "Let's assume that you have some key information that is critical to either your boss or your business partner in dealing with your client during negotiations. If you present it to your relevant partners before the negotiations, your information becomes instrumental in winning the negotiations; you will be viewed as proactive and giving the right amount of visibility. If you do not present the critical information beforehand, but after the fact, you could be blamed for acting defensively and full of excuses. It is all about timing in this ever-changing world. A piece of critical information presented at the right time can win your company an important deal."

Dealing with Change

The world is an ever-changing place and the pace of the change is accelerating. Our career or jobs will change at least 7 times in our lifetime. Future generations will be changing even more. Holding on to what we have, lifestyle, working style, existing technology, communication style is no longer realistic in this world.

One of my friends called one day and joked that the only people whose lives were not affected by this downturn in business are those on social security. I joked back; it won't be true for long when inflation hits the country.

The choice is up to you:

- Resist the change

- Accept the change

- Adapt to the change

- Embrace the change

At the end of the day, whether you are willing to change or not, your life is going to be different.

A positive attitude and the ability to anticipate the trend will enable you to embrace the change.

Each week, free yourself from your daily busy work and schedule four hours for research and gaining new knowledge. Your research will quickly show you the trends and tips that are helpful for your future.

Change comes with risks. Are you willing to take these risks? Are you in a position mentally and financially to take these risks?

One of my mentors told me, "Never run away from things; always run into something big for you." To embrace the change, you have to antici-pate it and adjust your career and life accordingly, learning new skills and moving into new fields. Make your assets inflation proof. Tips and ideas from experts are readily available. You just need to look for them and start to practice them today.

How to Talk to a Jerk

If you are not part of the solution, you are part of the problem. Jerks hardly ever bring solutions to the table; they just bring problems and complaints one after another.

If you run into notorious jerks in your life, both personal and professional, you are not alone. Dealing with jerks needs maturity and greater mental strength. Here are some helpful tips:

- Never lower yourself to the jerk's level. Try to elevate the conversation to your level, be professional, productive and solution driven.

- Hear his complaints and acknowledge that you heard him.

- Ask him for the solution (what needs to be done logically, not emotionally) and go over the consequences of his proposed solution or let him know you are going to evaluate his solution if you are not ready to go over his solution at this time.

- Stop the conversation if the jerk starts to bring you down to his level.

- Remind the jerk that you both are on the same team, you are not fighting a battle against him but you are here to collaborate.

- Stick to ideas. Do not let things get personal.

- Escalate the problem to his managers, let his managers know what happened and ask for help.

- Complain to the HR department, if appropriate.

Some of us are not comfortable confronting others. We tend to accept complaints and allow ourselves to be bullied. Then we complain to others. The problem is that jerks will continue to bully you and drive you in the wrong direction. You have to deal with damages and negative consequences. The longer they are allowed to bully you, the larger the problem becomes. The best way to deal with jerks is to confront them assertively, keep the conversation positive, try to build a collaborative spirit and discover a logical solution about the problems for which they are adamant.

Ballet vs. Hockey Game

My mentor Harry, former Chairman of the Board, once called me into his office, "Elizabeth, do you like ballet?" I said, "Of course, I love ballet!" Harry said, "How about hockey games?" "I have only watched a few times, but they seem quite exciting," I replied. Harry elaborated: "Running a business is like directing a ballet. You have planned the story line, plot and actions. You direct the show day in and day out, always making it perfect so everything seems smooth and effortless. As the director of the show, you give directions to your dancers. More importantly you provide the stage for them to perform, mentoring and coaching them to their highest potential. This is the highest level of leadership.

Hockey games are surely exciting. You chase after the puck. The puck is flying everywhere. The team is reacting as quickly as possible with many random actions. That is a game, not a business.

If you want to build a profitable business, you have to plan, direct, coach and mentor your people. Develop them into stars and provide the stage for them to perform to their fullest potential."

It has been years. I still remember his analogy of deep understanding about a high performance operation, and I try my best to direct a ballet, sometimes even in the middle of a hockey game.

Stress and Burnout

I still remember the topic from my first IBM English training class in 1997. The trainer, Brigit also taught at Stanford University. She was wise and knew the history of Silicon Valley technology inside and out, not only about companies but also about leaders. She talked about how Stanford University was started, but that was not what I remembered. What I remember today is avoiding burnout. She basically said that we were a group of outstanding talent that IBM chose to train, there would be a lot of challenges and long working hours in the future and we needed to watch for burnout in order to have a longer, and more sustainable, career.

That was the first time I ever heard about burnout. I was too shy to ask about burnout in front of the class, but was brave enough to ask her after the class. She explained burnout as: physical and mostly emotional exhaustion, resulting in a diminished sense of purpose, interests and accomplishments.

I was very lucky to know it at the beginning of my career. Fourteen years later, I called her and took her out to lunch, to thank her for the advice she gave me fourteen years ago. Brigit's advice not only improved my execution efficiency, but also helped me understand the stress of my team members and helped the organization cope with stress and burnout from daily execution. The software industry tends to be non-stop just like a mental assembly line.

Going to bed earlier, exercising regularly, getting adequate help and managing priorities are a few of the best ways to prevent burnout. In case you are overwhelmed by the mountains of tasks, watch out for signs of burnout:

- Emotional and physical exhaustion

- Withdrawal, do not even want to go to the office or read emails

- Inefficiency and lack of concentration

- Cynicism, nothing is serious enough, everything is wrong

- Emptiness

Take a few days off once you see these signs; seek help if you cannot recover from burnout on your own.

Pat used to have a long hard commute to work. The eight lanes of traffic were often stopped, not because of accidents, but because more cars were trying to enter the highway. She managed this stress by taking a longer route to work through the country and small towns. She was constantly moving while enjoying the flowers, colorful trees and beautiful scenery. The beauty of nature reduced the stress from her long daily commute on the eight lane gray concrete highway. I live in Silicon Valley, driving on scenic highway 280 adds 6 miles to my 60+ miles daily commute, but the scenery on highway 280 makes that 60+ miles more enjoyable than driving on Interstate 101.

A sense of humor also can save you from burnout. Unfortunately, I have almost no ability to crack a joke; however, I do have the ability to appreciate others' sense of humor and their clever jokes.

Great jokes put things in well-staged perspective. When you see the same thing from a different frame of reference, bright spots outshine the dark side of challenges and nonsense. Challenges are no longer scary or unbearable; nonsense becomes the raw material for you to distill wisdom and future best practices.

Laughing and singing often can also help you release stress. Pat laughs a lot and positive energy exudes from her laughter. Meditation also helps reduce stress.

Three Questions to Reduce Stress

Three questions I ask myself when I become stressed out or angry about something in family life or at the workplace:

1. Does it matter by the end of the day?

2. Does it matter by the end of the month?

3. Does it matter by the end of my life?

Most of these instances do not matter at all at the end of my life. These three questions take less than 8 seconds to ask, that 8 seconds of self-reflection shields me from many ugly blowouts, political fights and unnecessary stress. These three questions keep me zeroed in on the most important aspects of my life and career. I will not disperse my energy on trivial distractions.

What are your questions that help you to be more focused?

Procrastination

Procrastination is like an ostrich sticking its head in the sand to avoid seeing problems. The reality is, problems are there whether you see them or not. The load from procrastination is heavy enough; the cost of the emotional energy from procrastination sometimes can be overwhelming and take much more effort to finish the project.

Problems are magnified when you procrastinate. When making a snowman, you start with a snowball rolling it in the snow until it is a big fat bottom for your snowman. Although problems may start out small, if left unattended, they tend to get bigger and bigger and harder to solve. Dealing with change, talking to a jerk, stress and burnout all usually start out small, but can grow to become serious if not dealt with quickly.

What keeps you up at night? Often it is from tasks you know you should do, but have procrastinated about and now they may have gotten out of control. It is much easier to put out a small fire than a raging wildfire. As the old saying goes, "Don't put off until tomorrow, the job you should do today."

Office Politics

John asked me to speak to a group of young professionals about how to deal with office politics. I declined his request, "I don't think I am an expert in playing office politics."

That is true. Whenever I take over an organization, I declare three rules:

1. No negative politics

2. Respect and learn from each other

3. Deliver your promises

I will stop any activity that promotes negative politics and nip that behavior in the bud. However, I encourage my team to influence each other to focus on top priorities for our organization and company.

What is office politics? If you google it, you will be amazed how much energy is spent on this subject online, how many contradicting tips are out there. Many websites focus on providing tips and sharing crazy stories about office politics. Negative office politics are cancers in our society; they are pervasive and deadly for organizations and personal careers. Most of the tips from these websites are about dealing with negative office politics the type that I banned from my organizations.

Two articles that I highly recommend are:

"How to Win at Office Politics" by Beth Weissenberger, (http://www.businessweek.com/managing/content/feb2010/ca20100222_142589.htm)

"7 Habits to Win in Office Politics" (http://www.lifehack.org/articles/management/7-habits-to-win-in-office-politics.html)

In Beth Wiesenberger's article at BusinessWeek, she comments on office politics, "It's not about stabbing people in the back or doing absolutely anything to get ahead." She also says: "Office politics are about people interacting and building relationships to get things done. They're about getting ahead and accomplishing more, making you more fulfilled in your job. Office politics are what happens in a conversation, who wins in a conversation, who gets what they want, who says nothing, and who gets nothing..."

I agree with Beth's definition, office politics are about how to influence others and get things done for the company and your personal career.

The "7 Habits to Win in Office Politics" article provides you with useful tips to deflect negative politics:

1. Be aware you have a choice

2. Know what you are trying to achieve

3. Focus on your circle of influence

4. Don't take sides

5. Don't get personal

6. Seek to understand, before being understood

7. Think win-win

I suggest you think win-win-win. You may not always be able to achieve that in reality, but at least you have the intention and you have made a conscious decision to try to achieve that. If your company, your boss and your team win, your career wins too.

Managing Perceptions, Priorities and Personal Commitments (3P)

Let me quote the definition of execution again from The author of *Execution: The Discipline of Getting Things Done* by Larry Bossidy: "In its most fundamental sense, execution is a systematic way of exposing reality and acting on it."

Exposing reality is about compiling real status, progress and perceptions, acting on it is about calibrating your priorities and carrying out personal commitments.

Success is about calibrating and meeting commitments according to adjusted priorities. This statement sounds elegant and easy! However, in real life, it is the hardest thing to implement.

When we are dealing with a client, especially a powerful client who spends millions of dollars on your services, we often bend towards whatever way our client wishes. We make him happy in the beginning. If we cannot deliver our adjusted commitments, we fail our client's expectations. Bending without a reality check on our delivery capacity will set the client up for failure within his organization. In this case, we need to engage our client, align our limited resources to our client's most important priorities, and help him accomplish the most important commitments in a realistic timeline. Our client appreciates vendors who can provide a realistic timeline and deliver their quality commitments on time.

We often hear the phrase "Perception is reality". Perception is truth to the person who perceives it as we discussed in Chapter 1. Perception is the view others have from their own world, which could be very different from your inner view of yourself. To close the gap between other people's perceptions and your own personal views, you have to proactively construct and utilize the virtual boxes you created for the people whose perceptions are vital to your career progress. These virtual boxes will help you understand their priorities and value, open your mind to new ideas and out of box solutions which are better aligned with these stakeholders who can either accelerate or block your career development.

Asking straightforward questions can help you quickly align your priorities in this ever-changing world. When your boss piles you with more than three tasks, simply ask him one question, "Among all tasks, which do you want to finish first, second and so forth and why?" We do not have time to work on things that are no longer important to the organization or your boss. Never guess priorities, confirm his priority before you act!

Execution is not just about doing, it is about influencing relevant parties, managing their expectations and perceptions, adjusting priorities and personal commitments.

Homework

1.   List your rocks, pebbles, sand and water to fill your time jar.

2.   List the 10 most important tasks you want to do for this month.

3.   Build your time map, and color code your daily schedule according to these categories:

- Rocks - red
- Pebbles - green
- Sand - yellow
- Water - blue

4.   Are you scheduling your most important tasks during your most energetic time periods?

5.   What are your parallel projects that you can multitask?

6.   What are you going to do to manage stress and burnout?

7.   Design a plan to avoid procrastination.

8.   Decide how you will deal with jerks and office politics.

9.   What's your action plan to manage your 3Ps?

8

Mentoring and Networking

I was interviewed by Lily Chou, hostess on FM 96.1 in San Francisco. Lily asked me, "What was the first turning point in your career?" The answer jumped out of my mouth, "The day I met my mentor, Pat, who helped me see many opportunities and many paths that I never knew existed. Without Pat, I would not be who I am today!"

An excellent mentor passes on their wisdom, experiences and network to help you continue the legacy shared by both of you.

Why Do you Help me

In 1991, both Pat and Lou were my mentors. Lou was an outstanding businessman, teacher and retired Air Force Colonel who fought in World War II, the Korean War and the Vietnam War. The military sent him to Stanford University to become an engineer during the Korean War. He worked in research and development testing military equipment during the Vietnam War. When he retired, he started his own business working in mine safety. All through his life he met people who were illiterate. Quietly, Lou worked with these people, one-on-one, helping them to learn to read.

Pat developed a love of learning and volunteering throughout her life. When she took an early retirement from AT&T, she decided to fulfill a passion and teach adults to read, write and speak English.

Lou and Pat met at the Northern Nevada Literacy Council in Reno. Lou was a supervisor trainer for Laubach Literacy in America, one of the largest volunteer literacy organizations in America. He supervised Pat's development and training through the steps of tutor, trainer and supervisor trainer helping to certify her as a Laubach Literacy supervisory trainer also.

They enjoyed working together so they teamed up teaching literacy and English as Second Language (ESL) workshops throughout Nevada and northern California training other volunteers to become tutors and starting literacy organizations throughout the small towns as well as in the prison system.

Lou and Pat gave me the opportunity to speak in front of these workshops teaching the students about cultural differences. This was a win-win situation. It helped them understand the most effective ways to communicate with their future students and helped me enhance my presentation skills. They also invited me to fundraising events, political campaigns and other business and social events. I learned a tremendous amount from both of them.

Lou invited me to his beautiful ranch in the foothills of the Sierra mountains where I played with his goats and horses. Sitting on his front porch, drinking coffee, I asked him, "Lou, you never knew me before, why do you help me?" Lou smiled back, "I will not live forever. You are a good listener and learner, and more importantly, you work hard. Trust me; you have great potential to be very successful. One day, your success will be my legacy," he said patting my shoulder. He passed away a few years later.

The day he passed away, I felt that his mission was passed to me to continue his legacy and help others become successful, just as he helped me.

That five minute conversation with Lou completely changed my life's goal. Back in 1991, my goal in life was survival, to get through graduate school and earn my Ph.D. Lou elevated my goals from survival to success, then to a more noble and superior calling helping others.

Where to Find your Pat and Lou

Pat and Lou are great mentors. Many students who come to our seminars claim they do not have mentors and they never had one. They want to know where to find great mentors just like Pat and Lou.

It is hard to find Pat and Lou. I was lucky. I also have 20+ other mentors such as: Beth Smith, Joseph Chen, Harry V., Jim G., Larry Chang, Wes Hom, Milton Chang, George Koo and my neighbors Bob S. and Tiffany.

Mentors are everywhere; they might sit next to your desk, be your former boss, your neighbor, even a mailman.

I run into my mailman on the elevator at 8:00 AM once or twice a week. He has a great smile. I always say hi when I see him. He told me one day, "A lady with a beautiful smile brightens rainy days. A good smile goes a long way." His big smile reminds me to smile during stressful situations. It relaxes people around me and projects positive energy.

Who is a Great Mentor

Mentors are people who have the ability to share their life experiences, lessons and knowledge honestly. They exude positive professionalism. Good mentors have big hearts. They appreciate differences in people, are willing to work with you and take a personalized approach to solve your unique career related issues and provide guidance. Good mentors are excellent in constructing solutions according to your situation.

Mentors do not have to be there for you all the time. I only talk to some of my mentors once or twice. Some of them gave me advice only once many years ago.

Excellent mentors open their network for you, provide you with resources and people who have special expertise. Their past experience can become a preview of what is in front of you. They broaden your horizons and elevate your goals just like Lou did for me.

Excellent mentors provide you with non-threatening and constructive feedback. One-on-one meetings with your mentor are the best opportunity to share insight and deep motivations that drive your behavior. You can be honest with your trusted mentor; together you two can diagnose your problems and come up with customized solutions to your problems.

My mentors offer me many great techniques that they use to improve productivity and communication. Larry Chang taught me to have weekly conversations about goals and feedback with my bosses. Pat taught me how to engage others in planning, gaining group support from the beginning. Allen taught me how to become more focused and strategic, delegating responsibilities in order to be more effective and successful.

Most mentors exude professionalism, personal drive and discipline. They are devoted to helping others be more successful and build a better community. When I am with them, I never feel that they have their own personal interests in mind. I feel elevated. I become a better person and better leader each time.

How to Approach Mentors

If your company does not have a formal mentoring program, you are on your own. Many non-profit organizations such as Ascend and Mount Jade American Association (MJAA) provide mentoring programs. You can join these organizations, participate in a few mentoring events and find someone you respect and are willing to ask to become your mentor.

Approaching a great mentor takes courage. I called the number for ESL training at the bus stop and found Pat and Lou. I ran into Larry and Buck at conferences and simply asked them on the spot. I had teas and dinners with my neighbors or chatted with them in front of our recycle bins. I asked our chairman of the board to mentor me after a board meeting. I walked to the parking lot with my second line manager Bev, discovered that we worked at the same research institute and she became my mentor at IBM.

There is an old Chinese proverb, "When the student is ready, the teacher will appear." Students simply need to ask.

How to Build a Long Lasting Mentoring Relationship

I have only met with Josephine Chang twice since I left IBM in 2000. Jo became a distinguished IBM Fellow and VP of Research. She was heading the IBM China R&D Center and expanded IBM China R&D Center significantly. Two years ago, Jo came back to the United States to lead. I went to see her at the beautiful Almaden Research Center where I used to work one day a week.

Jo was energetic as usual. She was very excited about a few cutting edge research projects and giving talks around the world. I asked her why she picked me as a mentee. Jo looked at me across the lunch table, "You were open to my suggestions. You put forth effort to try them out and then came back for more suggestions. You volunteered for our groups, you demonstrated the ability to influence others and make things happen."

My other mentor, ex-boss Jim said, "You are like a student; you want to learn and to try. You look for advice proactively."

I have been a mentor for many years. I like mentees who do exactly what Jo and Jim said. A good mentee must listen and try on advice from mentors.

Respect Mentors' Time and Advice

Mentors give their time and energy to you for free; mentees should show their respect. Following the advice and assignments from mentors is essential. Most mentors are very successful and busy, mentees should respect mentors' time. Do not demand too much of their time.

I had 15 minute monthly meetings with my executive mentors at IBM. I was in and out within 15 minutes, asked my questions and reported back my progress. I was able to keep that simple and effective mentorship for years with Beth, VP of a different product line, and the rising star at IBM, who was much younger and more accomplished than I was.

Lunch meetings are very effective with my other mentors. I like to take my mentors to lunch. Parallel communication with my mentors can get us into deep and honest discussion quickly. Delicious meals and good environment make it more enjoyable. I have had quarterly lunch with my group of mentees for several years.

Others play tennis with their mentors. John Chambers, CEO of Cisco, used to play tennis with Dr.

An Wang frequently. That experience might have influenced his career as CEO of Cisco.

I go skiing and shopping with some of my mentees. Some of them have become my best friends. Some of my mentees asked me to be their start up advisers and board members.

Developing meaningful activities will bring the relationship to the next level. Although Pat and I are not living in the same city, I call Pat before I get to my office most mornings. We write blogs and this book together, collaborate using Google docs each week. Once I had Pat on the phone while I was teaching a class. She flew to California for a week to co-teach our class at Stanford University.

Respect and meaningful activities will help you build a long lasting mentoring relationship and maybe more meaningful business relationships. It should be a win-win relationship so both mentor and mentee win.

Find a Supporter within your Company

Mentors are essential, supporters within your company are critical to your near-future career advancement. Four years ago, Larry and I were on the panel at an MJAA mentoring event. He suggested everyone find a supporter within their company.

A supporter is someone who is very influential within your group or company; someone who believes in your capability and has a trusting relationship with you. Confidentiality is required for all mentoring relationships; there is absolutely no room to compromise in this situation. You have to treat every piece of advice, information and insight from your supporter as absolutely confidential. A trusting relationship remains when everything is confidential.

Supporters are critical to your immediate future because they give you needed organization knowledge including advice on corporate politics, insight and opportunities to which you have no visibility or exposure. They are powerful or influential enough that they can point you in the right direction for opportunities for promotions and career shifts. I have had many supporters during my career. Turning points in my career were given by my supporters.

Multipliers vs. Diminishers

I have worked for some highly intelligent managers. Some are the best technologists in the industry. My team members loved to talk to them. We were often motivated, inspired and came up with new ideas during conversations just from being around them. You may have had the same experience. When these kinds of leaders walk into a room, light bulbs go on over people's heads, ideas flow and problems get solved. These are the leaders who inspire employees to stretch themselves to deliver results that surpass expectations.

Liz Wiseman, author of best seller *Multipliers: How the Best Leaders Make Everyone Smarter* called them the multipliers. Multipliers do not want to be perceived as the smartest people in the room; they want people to feel smarter after spending time in their presence. In fact, they are the wisest people in the room.

There are other types of leaders who always want to be the smartest people in whatever rooms they enter, no matter if they are an expert of the discussed subjects or not. These types of leaders make others feel stupid, stressed, less energetic and less creative. Instead of being inspired to solve tough issues, the team tried hard to follow their smart questions and wisdom regardless of the subject.

I once worked with such a leader who asked more than ten questions on any trivial matter, making me feel stupid for not knowing such finite details about trivial matters. Yes it is true, the devil is in the details, but really it did not matter whether I knew the details or not because the matter is so trivial. It was not critical to our business or execution at all.

Liz Wiseman called these types of leader's diminishers, who drain intelligence, energy and capability from the ones around them.

Liz Wiseman also showed how multipliers can have a resoundingly positive and profitable effect on organizations—getting more done with fewer resources, developing and attracting talent and cultivating new ideas and energy to drive organizational change and innovation.

A mentor who coaches you and also makes you feel smarter and more confident each time you talk to him will be an excellent coach for your career. You can also learn to become a multiplier from him. A multiplier can be a true leader who can grow his team and channel creativity, talent and passion from the team to achieve a mission impossible for diminishers.

Networking

Networking has become very popular in recent years because of the ever-popular social networks: LinkedIn and Facebook. Technology helps us expand and maintain our network much easier than pre-web times. However even with this Internet aid, you are still the person who attracts and builds your network.

Orthogonal Networking

My friend complained to me, "I have been seeing the same friends in the same professions for 20 years, they are my competitors in the job market, and I am not motivated to network with them!"

I sort of agree with her. I suggested she try something different, something I called "Orthogonal Networking". Instead of networking with the group of people who have the same professions, network with people who are in the same field, but in different roles. For example: If you are an engineer, try to network with an accountant, a sales person or marketing person, and vice versa. If you are a controller, you might want to network with a venture capitalist (VC), CEO or another executive.

These friends in orthogonal roles know what is going on in their companies and will recommend you for the openings in their company without feeling threatened.

Your Network

In 1998, I attended a manager meeting at IBM. One of the Senior Executives said, "The 20th century is a super hero century. One person's great effort can make a huge difference, one person can be hugely successful. But, the 21st century is a century of collaboration, no single super hero can be as successful as a group of great talent. No one can grasp and fully interpret the over-whelming amount of technology and information. One can only be an expert on a limited number of subjects. If you want to be successful, collabo-rate with each other, build trust so that you can quickly exchange information, assemble SWAT teams and conquer future complex challenges."

Ten years ago I paid $1000 to attend a conference in San Francisco. Years went by, the only thing I remembered was that the speaker said, "You are the average person in your network. If you only have junior people in your network, you won't be able to quickly advance your business and career because you have no one to learn from, get constructive feedback and advice from."

That was $1000 well spent.

We all have our own circle of friends and networks. These circles of people influence our lives every moment. We influence their lives too. My network taught me so much. I avoided many mistakes. I found so many shortcuts.

Five Circles of People Around you

Draw 5 circles, and write down names in the circles. When you look at names in between these circles, your network is on paper.

- Core Circle (family and best friends, providing emotional support)

- Inner Circle (business partners and people who give you professional and business advice)

- Buddy Circle (People you do things with: run, ski, dance, camp, fellow board members or committee members)

- Peer Circle (people you work with, spend 8+ hours each weekday)

- Social Circle (LinkedIn, Facebook, professional conferences and organizations, people you see 1-2 times a year or a life, but share information and keep in touch, people you will get resources from or market your product to.

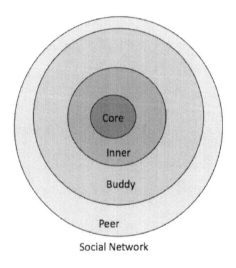

Social Network

Five Circles of Your Network

We have been talking about these circles since 2004. Now Google+ has implemented network circles; we view that as a good validation of our concepts.

Core Circle

Family and best friends are in your Core Circle. They influence you the most . They may have high expectations of you or just give up on you. They can support you when you are down or they can drain your emotional energy completely. This circle of people needs management and support from you to be fully functional as a positive force.

As the old saying goes, "Behind every success- ful man, there is a great woman." In fact, every successful career is supported by several people. Between kids and career, there just is not enough time to do everything well. Many Asian families hire live-in nannies or have grandparents living with them to cook and take care of young chil- dren.

Kevin had a dysfunctional family when he was very young. His parents fought every day. When he was 14, he convinced his parents to allow him to live with his grandparents who were a loving and caring couple. He chose his friends carefully, only hanging out with positive kids from happy families. He married well and now enjoys a happy family life. Several times, he had to leave nega- tive friends and make new friends. Kevin told me that he was emotionally tired and he could not afford to be with anyone who was negative.

Inner Circle

Your mentors, advisers and business partners are your inner circle. This circle is completely under your control. You do not need Kevin's courage to swap people out of your inner circle. However, you need to constantly seek the right people for your inner circle and constantly renew your inner circle as you grow. This is the most critical circle of all five. People in this circle can either break you or make you successful quickly. You should be the most junior person in this circle.

Buddy Circle

Buddy Circle is the source of pure pleasure, stress relief and personal artistic or spiritual expression. It keeps your body going:

- Rock climbing
- Skiing
- Golfing
- Dancing
- Shopping
- Singing
- Photography
- Painting

People in your Buddy Circle seldom have anything to do with your current professional life.

Communicating with your Circles at Right Frequency

Lunchtime, evening and weekends are the best time to interact with your network. We suggest you to have at least 6 lunches and one dinner with your network per month, attend at least social one event or technical meet-up.

Emails and social network sharing are excellent ways to keep your network engaged and informed, however, it is best to keep it at a weekly basis to avoid spamming your network.

How to Find the Right Business Partners

Business partners must satisfy the following criteria:

1) Trust each other with money and reputation

2) Share same dreams and goals

3) Be flexible to collaboration and adjust roles in the venture

4) Have a strong drive to be the best in the class

5) Keep win-win in mind, both partners must succeed

6) The venture must either be profitable and solve a real problem or nonprofit to better the world or community

7) Must be multipliers to each other

You should have one lunch with your inner circle people per week and two lunches to look for new inner circle members per month.

Homework

1.   Name three or more mentor candidates and determine what you want to learn from these mentors.

2.   Name three or more candidates who may become your supporters.

3.   Make plans to approach these mentors and supporters.

4.   Name three people to mentor, identify one mentee who will be mentored regularly.

5.   Define your network diagram; put people in your five circles.

6.   Identify three network organizations that you are interested in joining and volunteer at one network organization.

7.   Add 5 connections to your LinkedIn network.

9

Build your Team

What is your Team?

When people talk about a team, they generally talk about a group of people who work for them. Is that all?

I define the team with a much broader boundary. A team is a group of people that a leader needs to attract, motivate, grow, mentor or to be mentored. It consists of advisers and experts from whom you can seek advice and execution, members who can validate and carry out your plans. Sometimes, one member can be an advisor and an execution team member at the same time.

My team concept is a complete team, like a startup company. All members are involved and engaged with real projects and activities. The team consists of:

- Advisers

- Partners

- Working members

You can be the leader of your own team and become a member of other people's teams. A team can make or break a leader and a leader can make or break a team.

There are many excellent leaders around us as well as in history, who had distinctive leadership styles. Regardless of how they lead their teams, successful leaders share some critical traits:

- Good teacher and mentor skills with teachable points of view

- Strong shared team values, principles and business ideas

- Clear individual ownership

- Delegation and empowerment skills

Most of the best leaders are good teachers. They devote a lot of their time teaching or coaching team members. They inspire their teams by being good role models. This is a more successful leadership style than leaders who force their ideas on their team members.

Good leaders share their strong values and instill uniform values across their team. No one can make every decision for their team every day, if someone tried, I guarantee a failure due to demotivating the team. Some smart first time managers or entrepreneurs believe in themselves more than their team members. They have tight control over the decision making process which often demotivates their team. It makes the team afraid to take risks when they lose decision making capabilities.

A unified, strong team value is the most critical factor for a successful team. It enables a team to make decisions that are consistent. Most good leaders share their plans, and more importantly share their business ideas. Sharing ideas behind each plan with team members inspires them to be more creative, which brings more profit to the business and a great product. Some great leaders enlarge their team concept to their customers, sharing their business ideas or intentions with their customers. Customer feedback becomes their idea factory and source of inspiration.

Clear ownership is the base of delegation and empowerment. When people have clear ownership of a project, they are more motivated, creative and productive. They care about their professional reputation and their results. The leader should take risks with the team members and give credit when things go well. Trust among team members strengthens ownership and furthers empowerment.

Clear ownership should not generate solos. A leader of the team should generate synergy among team members in order to achieve their common goals.

Rewarding yourself and your team members will motivate and energize you and keep you engaged. We devote Chapter 10 to rewarding people with:

- Praise

- Money

- Shares of business

Teams and team members are not randomly selected; rather they are selected based on your career goals. You should join teams and participate in projects which can provide more skills and experiences for your career advancement. You should also select team members who can provide complementary skills for your team. It would be great if they can align their career goals with your projects. A win-win relationship certainly will be long lasting.

Five Levels of Delegation

When we talk about ownership, delegation and empowerment, many people ask how much should they delegate and empower to their team members. How much of ownership, delegation and empowerment should they expect from their managers?

The best classification of delegation I have read appeared in an "Executive Leadership" publication (www.execleadership.com). The 5 levels of delegation provide clear definitions and expectations.

Level 1 Delegation: Do exactly what I have asked you to do.

The manager already researched options, defined directions and determined a course of action. The team member is asked to do exactly what the manger wants. The team member cannot deviate from the instruction, and must report back the outcome of his action

Level 2 Delegation: Research the topic and report back research results.

The manager would like to explore a new option, the team member needs to investigate details and get back to the manager. The manager will provide more instruction and draw possible options.

Level 3 Delegation: Research the topic and outline possible options. The manager provided direction, asked the team members to research and come up with a few possible solutions and a recommendation. If the manager agrees with the recommendation, the team member will move forward with his recommendation.

Level 4 Delegation: Make a decision and then tell the manager what you did. The manager trusts the team member with their research, options and decision. The manager just wants to be in the loop, so as to not be surprised.

Level 5 Delegation: Make whatever decision you think is the best, no need to report back to manager. The manager completely trusts the team member's judgment and execution capability, or the task is well-defined, not super critical or strategic.

These five levels of delegation are based on clear ownership and the nature of the task. Level 5 delegation is pretty rare. If you are given level 5 delegation on strategic projects, be sure to lower it to level 4, keep your manager in the loop! He will not be surprised, but he will be supportive when there is an issue!

Microwave Leaders

Many leaders are proud of their ability to attend to details and put their team members into action. It certainly is a great leadership trait. I also witness many leaders who put high pressure on their team every minute asking for meaningless details. Their goal is not about moving toward a strategic direction, but about control. By directing their teams to do unnecessary tasks, they satisfy a personal craving to control every single detail. They remind me of a microwave oven. A microwave oven generates heat by spinning water molecules back and forth but it doesn't move them anywhere.

Be an inspiring leader, not a microwave oven which kills individual creativity and passion. Be a goal and result oriented leader, not a heat generating microwave oven.

Teaching Skiing

My two boys started skiing at 4 years-old, since their father and I love the sport. When my older son turned four, we were so excited and took him with us to the mountains. We put him in ski class with tears.

One hour later, my husband decided to check on our son. To his surprise, he found my four-year-old on the lift all by himself. How dangerous! My husband took him out of class immediately.

I asked him if he wanted to ski with Mommy instead of going back to the class. The four-year-old loved the idea. We put him on the lift with us and jumped off the lift with him. At the top of the hill, I put him in-between my skis, we laughed all the way down to the bottom of the hill.

He enjoyed it so much, swooping down the slopes while still under the protection of his mother. I lifted him up when we ran into bumps or when we had a sharp turn or a stop. I enjoyed teaching him to ski and still remember how little he was when he was four years old.

The second day, I tied a strap around his waist and held him from the back. On the third day, holding the same pole, we skied side by side. By the end of the third day, I asked him, "Is Mommy a good teacher?" He said with his head high, "I am good!" That was the best answer I ever heard!

As parents or leaders of businesses, the best results occur when you grow your children or your team members in a way that at the end of day they have built up self-confidence and ability. They learn from you without even realizing it. You are there providing a safety net and guidance according to their skill levels. You bring them to the game more quickly with strength and intensity.

Six years have passed and my son is now ten years old. He can ski half pipes, forward and backward, on the slopes of Double Diamond. He goes places with my friends who are experts; he has grown far beyond my capability. I am so proud of him. Whether he remembers or not, the very first time he enjoyed skiing was when I held him between my skis.

Our children and our team's successes become part of our legacy even though we never ask for credit or payback, witnessing their accomplishments is one of the most satisfying moments of our lives.

Retaining and Building a Strong Team

This question from one of our readers, was asked at a real interview for the first line manager job:

"You are a manager and there are a few engineers in your group. They are all smart and competitive engineers. One day one engineer comes to you and says he has been working in this area for a long time and he wants to transfer to a different group and try something different. What does it mean? How do you respond? Suppose that the engineer finally left and went to another group. Sooner or later another engineer comes to the manager again and wants to leave for similar reasons. What should you do?"

My answer to the reader was: "As the manager of the group, you should always understand your employee's 1, 2, and 5 year goals. Assign them tasks accordingly. If you have a very competitive group, you should ask them to spend 5% -10% of their time investigating new technologies, cross training each other, trying to initiate new projects for the group and pushing them to re-invent themselves to keep up with industry. You can motivate the team better if they get your support in expanding their technical horizons.

As the manager of the group, you should also go out of your way to find additional projects for the group and expand the group's responsibility by providing help or advice to other groups. Providing advice to other groups will improve the credibility of your employees and give them more visibility and promotion opportunities. You will earn your employee's respect and trust as well as credit from upper management for your initiative, collaboration and employee development."

Pat's answers to the same question: "Rule number one at Illinois Bell was, 'A good manager promotes his people.' I agree with Elizabeth's answer. To be an effective team you need to get to know your employees and their personal goals. Meet with them individually as well as in the work group. Share the goals of the group and what your boss expects from this group. It is important that each employee knows and understands what is expected of him. Find projects that will help your employees learn new things and excel at their work. You want them to succeed. You want to be able to recommend them for promotions. Their success is your success. If you have followed Elizabeth's advice, you have your team cross-trained so you will have a qualified person to backfill when you lose your experienced engineer."

You are a Star

I attended a Women in Technology (WITI) conference at Santa Clara Convention Center. I was a new first line manager at IBM Santa Teresa Lab. The whole conference went by very quickly. I felt like a sponge soaking up all the information floating around me. Many tips later left me. However, one tip stands out in my memory and I continuously use it today.

During one of the breakout sessions, an executive from one of the high tech companies went to the whiteboard and drew an irregular star. She turned around and said, "You are a star!" She pointed to the star on the whiteboard. "Your strengths and weaknesses make you a unique star." Then she drew another bigger star on top of the first star. She looked at us. "You have to focus on enhancing your strengths at the same time you diminish your weaknesses, in order to become a bigger star."

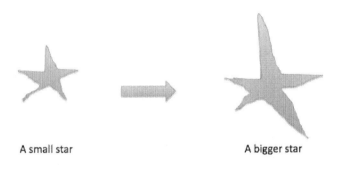

A small star   A bigger star

A small start becomes a bigger star in a different shape by enhancing strengths

"You are a star" is a powerful opening statement in most career building sessions and performance review meetings. It puts strength and weakness in perspective, both manager and employee or mentor and mentee can look at strength and weakness in an objective manner.

A star   A ball without strengths

A smaller star becomes a small ball without any
strength by focusing on weaknesses

Focusing on weaknesses only turns a star into a
ball. When an employee becomes a ball, he will
lose his strength and confidence. He will lose motivation; he will lose his personal identity. Once a
ball forms the star disappears.

An excellent manager should help the team identify unique strengths and turn everyone into a
star of his own - a star with confidence, strength,
talent and unique skills. These stars will follow
the leader and a star team will produce outstanding results for the business.

Being Challenged or Managed

My friend lost his job recently and has been
actively interviewing for a new one.

Last month he came out of an interview and
called his best friends, telling us how excited he
was. He felt challenged by the hiring manager, by
his energy, vision and ambition. We all hoped he

would get his dream job. But he did not. One of the stakeholders did not approve hiring him. We felt very sorry for him.

He went to another interview a few days ago, another good opportunity. We were all excited for him and kept our fingers crossed. He called me after his interview; his voice was low, filled with sadness. He said he felt he would be managed not challenged by the hiring manager during the interview.

How sad! Being managed and not challenged! A creative mind that is challenged generates excellent ideas. A great leader sets the bar high, exudes high energy and challenges and inspires his employees.

A good manager could use a matter-of-fact attitude, gather all the facts about all the candidates, compare their strengths and weaknesses and then make their decision. Yes, he could get the most qualified employee, but might not get a super-charged employee, an innovative mind and productive and creative solution generator.

Collaboration and Leadership

The first time I really heard the word collaboration was when I still worked at IBM. One of the Sr. VPs spoke to us about the difference between the 20th and 21st centuries. He referred to the

20th century as the century of super heroes, who either destroyed or saved the world, companies and communities. Due to the vast amount of information and accelerated rate of information addition and exchange, it would be impossible for one person to digest the vast amount of information and provide penetrating messages beyond the noise of the ever growing information universe. Then the 21st century became the century of team collaboration, that groups of super heroes would work together, utilize their expertise and strength, process information that they could best understand, provide their expert strategy and methodology, flawlessly execute the team's plan and reach the ultimate goal.

Since the turn of the century, the buzz word collaboration has become popular as well as frequently abused, and it is rising fast to the top of the list of not to use political vocabulary. Some people used it as an excuse to avoid responsibility and others used it to postpone making hard decisions. It was used as a place to hide behind fellow workers in case the project did not work out.

Note that I did not use Collaboration vs. Leadership as the title. In an effective organization, leadership and collaboration are best friends. They should appear hand in hand all the time. When new responsibility appears, usually it is tough and challenging. A real leader never uses collaboration to shy away from these tough moments. Some call it the MOT (moment of truth.) A real leader is someone who is courageous enough to take on challenges and walk on churning political undercurrents, assuming responsibility, gathering the team's input, making the tough decisions and leading the team forward.

Leading a team forward needs synergy. Synergy comes from inspiration and team collaboration. A rocket to the moon was inspired by the president, implemented by many highly skilled scientists, engineers and supporting teams, materials and parts around the world. Collaboration enables great endeavors and complex modern technology production. When three people are randomly drafted together, their goals and efforts may not be aligned and skills may not be complimentary to each other. Their efforts can actually cancel each other out, you would see "1+1+1 <3" or even "1+1+1<0". When "1+1+1>3" happens, real collaboration is at work. When sparks of synergy turn into flaming fire, "1+1+1 >4 or more"!

A real leader makes tough calls and energizes teams around him via collaboration. Only the ones who master the leadership as well as collaboration can accomplish many impossible missions with their teams.

Respect your Team

During one of my SVP jobs, I wanted to establish a trusting and respectful work environment. More than twenty outstanding individuals were promoted out of 200+ professionals. The normal way was to send out one email announcing the promotion. I thought long and hard about this and decided to use promotion announcements to convey a message showing how every person was respected because of his accomplishments, and more importantly, who he was as an individual. I asked managers to write promotion announcements, then ask the employees to collaborate via Google doc, insert life stories, family pictures and favorite quotes to complete the promotion of the day announcements.

Some of them shared their brief biography, some of them shared one life event that changed their life, such as a layoff experience that changed their life goals which made them better people and helped realize their family values.

Only one promotion announcement was sent out per day, making each person stand out as the super star of the day. I got the chance to know my best people during that period of time, so did the organization. Some of my employees told me that even though they worked with several of these people for many years, they never knew much about them.

This campaign completely changed our culture and team dynamic. Lack of respect and trust was eliminated; people were respected for their accomplishments, unique talent and special skills. Their family often participated in drafting part of the promotion announcement. That certainly made the family proud and engaged with our company.

Where do Leaders Get their Directions

No one is born with directions. Most leaders usually develop their vision through years of experience in conducting business, utilizing technology, building teams and organizations. Leaders most likely are surrounded by an intelligent team, which provides data, opinions and options. What separates the leader from the regular team member is the unique ability to simplify the situation, take the risk, identify the direction, validate and recalibrate the direction with his team along the way toward the target.

In the early 20th century, it would take a much longer time to gain data to make bold decisions and take dramatic directions. Some leaders had guts to take risks and did something others would not dare to attempt.

During the Information Age in the 21st century, everything is more complicated. Guts alone are not enough for leaders to identify the most optimal directions for the team. They need data, expert opinions and reality validation from a team. And they need it in a record short time.

Leaders use Return on Investment (ROI) and Net Present Value (NPV) to evaluate their opportunities. They also check if the opportunity fits the following criteria:

- Company vision

- Marketing strategy

- Sales strategy

- Product road map

- Fitness to current product user experience and product offering

- Workforce skill sets/execution capacity

- Unique value to users

These criteria certainly will filter out noise and provide leaders with a few final choices. Now the guts will help leaders to take risks and make the final call.

Leaders do not get their ideas from thin air, they finalize their directions from their team's collective intelligence.

A Blender vs. an Engine

A blender has sharp blades and always moves very fast. It spins and forces everything around it into a high speed circular movement; it breaks everything into finite pieces.

An engine moves one direction and drives everyone on board in that direction.

The question is, are you a blender or an engine to your organization?

Are you a sharp leader who drives everyone around you crazy, chops up their ideas and sense of direction? Or are you the engine, who drives your team in one direction and helps them reach their goals?

A blender leader emails his team 10 times a day, each email contains different best practices in the industry. You will never be sure what he really wants. When you propose an idea to him, he always can identify the flaws in your proposal and make you feel stupid or not capable of communicating at his level of intelligence. He values quick ideas and fast execution of his ideas. Mostly, fast execution generates half-baked solutions and discrete products (not integrated into your overall product offerings). He does not understand much about day in and day out consistent execution toward a well thought out product road map. A blender leader always wants to be the smartest person in the room.

What if your boss is a blender who drives you crazy and you cannot get anything accomplished? Pat suggests you find another job. There is no way to change your boss, only he can do that. However, you can certainly try to influence him. Before you give up, try to establish some agreement with him that will allow you to be insulated from his sharp blades so you can concentrate on your tasks.

Insulating your team from your blender boss is a challenging task. You have to sacrifice your sanity in order to be in his churning inside circle. Another strategy to deal with that boss is not jumping into that blender! Watching him outside of the blender might be better for you. The price is that you will not be in his dynamic inside circle. Rewards are your sanity, mental energy and a productive team who accomplishes their milestones without chasing their own tails.

If you are suffering from a blender boss, I agree with Pat, find another job.

I also worked for an engine boss who inspired me to direct the team toward well thought out directions. We accomplished a tremendous amount of work under his leadership without chasing daily ideas to please him.

Homework

1.   Identify real projects you either want to lead or join.

2.   Identify your team members.

3.   Identify the teams in which you want to participate.

4.   Identify your unique roles in each team.

5.   Build teachable points of view and share your business ideas with your team members.

10

Reward and Motivate Frequently

Love Yourself

Many people asked me, "How do you motivate yourself?" I asked back, "How do you motivate others? Are you positive or critical in general?"

Pat and I have talked about this topic many times. One morning, Pat just said in a very point blank way, "You need to love yourself!" Many high-achievers are extremely critical of themselves. They frequently beat themselves up for the most minor mishaps. They never feel they have done enough to make themselves and their families proud.

Being introspective is not a bad thing, indeed, it helps you avoid being aloof and keeps you working harder towards your goals. Being overly critical of yourself, however, plays an opposite role when

you start to blame yourself for every unfortu-
nate event in your life. It becomes a heavy load
that drags you deeper and deeper into a sea of
hopelessness and despair. You may spend all your
efforts fighting the darkness and end up drown-
ing in depression.

Depression kills your spirit, creativity and dreams.
Life without dreams and hope is like living in
Azkanban[1]. Over time, you turn into a dementor[2],
sucking hope and joy out of the people around
you. Love yourself if you want to be a source of
happiness, courage and inspiration.

How do overly critical high-achievers learn to
love themselves and get out of the dark and cold
Azkanban? Write down your accomplishments and
happy moments. Read them every morning when
you get up. Look into the mirror and smile at the
image looking back. Look at the positive side of
each event during the day. Stop and smell the
roses, enjoy the small positive things around you.
By the end of the day, share your roses instead of
thorns with your friends and family. Reward yourself as you accomplish your goals, celebrate with
your friends and family and share your happiness
with people you love. They will be sincerely happy
for you.

As we travel life's long journey experiencing successes and failures, we all need someone who

---

1   Prison for wizards in Harry Potter books. Rowling, J.K. Harry
Potter and the Sorcerer's Stone. London: Bloomsburg. 1997.
2   Prison guard for Azkanban in Harry Potter books. Rowling,
J.K. Harry Potter and the Sorcerer's Stone. London: Bloomsburg.
1997.

will give us unconditional love. That person should be you first. Instead of being our own worst enemy, be our own best friend and biggest supporter. Love yourself unconditionally, dream about your bright future, exude positive energy, light up a room when you walk in, brighten a conversation when you join a group, put laughter on the dinner table, smile at happy events, laugh at your own dismal failures.

As Pat said, "Love yourself!" Care for yourself enough that you live your life to your fullest potential and have fun!

Reward yourself

There are numbers of books and talks about motivating yourself. You can set your alarm, get out of bed at 5AM, run 5 miles each day and work 14 hours each day. How long will that last?

Yes, a few people can work like that for their lofty career goals. Most of us cannot. We need to recharge, we need to be rewarded at incremental milestones. Our emotional engine needs fuel, needs to be satisfied when we reach these milestones.

Pat and I constantly reward ourselves. We reward ourselves to make our achievements a long lasting memory. When we finished our first Stanford class, we went for a massage and a fancy dinner at my country club. When we finished the

2nd whole day class, I bought a new mixer for myself, and gifted my old one to a friend.

My favorite recharging activities are:

- Enjoy my garden - playing with my flowers and vegetables
- Go to the beach with my family, taking their pictures
- Play golf with my family
- Ski with my family
- Watch classic movies
- Dance with my friends

Other ideas for rewarding yourself:

- Buy your favorite books
- Make chocolate chip cookies (easy and delicious!)
- Dip berries in chocolate
- Take a day off, watch DVDs
- Ask your partner for a massage
- Take a bubble bath
- Blend your favorite drink
- Download a couple of songs

- Spend time with a loved one
- Get your favorite take-out
- Give yourself some quiet time with a book or music
- Take a day off from any goal activities
- Take a nap
- Watch your favorite TV shows
- Do something you love
- Window shop (can be dangerous!)
- Go to a museum
- Have a cup of tea
- Have a glass of wine with dinner

Life should be enjoyed each day. The saddest thing would be, when you retire, to have never enjoyed yourself. You may have lived your life, but never experienced life much; you are still a kid living in an aging body.

When you are young, you may not have the ready cash to travel first class. Do not stay home feeling sorry for yourself. Travel third class and see all the same sights. The Eiffel Tower looks the same to someone who travels economy class as those who travel first class.

Money, Time and Relationships

To many of us, when we were at college, money was the most important element of our lives. We needed it to pay bills and buy things we liked. Many of us worked not so glamorous jobs, exchanging time for money. We learned tremendously from that life experience. We treasured money.

After a few years of stable jobs, we earned more money. But the money was never enough for us to feel secure. We worked more. We worked day and night. Then we discovered we had no time to spend with those most important to us. When sitting next to our children, we checked our messages and replied to our boss' emails at all hours. One of my friend's son yelled at her one day, "You love your phone more than you love me!" She was physically with her family but her mind drifted away to her work. She was never with her family 100%.

Some of us found we had to make appointments with our spouses just to spend some time alone. Then we became smarter. We discovered how to use money to buy time. We pay for cooks, cleaning services and babysitters. We pay drivers to drive our kids around. We get private lessons for our children.

One Sunday morning, I opened my laptop as usual to work on some projects. A newspaper cartoon was taped to my screen, "Are you more available to your devices than to your family? Are you sure? Then why is this message taped to your computer?" My son signed his name to the newspaper.

I turned around; my son looked at me with a big smile. I closed my laptop and spent a memorable Sunday with my family at the beach.

While sitting on the beach watching a beautiful sunset, I realized a funny circle I went through: using time to earn money when we did not have money, then using money to buy time when we ran short on time. However, time and money become insignificant when our most important relationships are hurting.

A few years ago, I heard a story on the radio, "There are five balls in your life: health, relationships, career, wealth and belief. Health and relationships are glass balls that are hard to repair when you drop them. Career, wealth and beliefs are rubber balls that will bounce back if you drop them." Never drop the glass balls.

How much time and money do you invest in your most important relationships? What are you going to do differently in the coming days and years? A beautiful healthy relationship is the engine of most long lasting happy memories and most valuable engine to help you through tough times.

Life Experience

My long lost friend, May, called me out of the blue. Three minutes into the conversation, we talked about life. Life is made up of events. Although individual events seem accidental, woven together they form relationships and experiences which impact how you feel about yourself. In that sense, nothing is accidental. Everything intertwines impacting your future, ultimately creating your present and future life experiences. May joked that there were two types of people in the world. One type creates stories and the other listens to stories. Story creators are full of surprises and new initiatives, their life experiences are exciting. Listeners get excited just observing them, wanting to be included in these stories.

At lunchtime, I was five minutes' early. While waiting for my friend I noticed a table with four ladies talking and laughing. What a happy table! I could not help noticing that one lady was radiant with happiness and excitement. That made her so beautiful and attractive. She was the story creator naturally drawing her friends to her. She smiled and talked to the waiter. The waiter walked away with a contented smile. I was no longer bored waiting.

I thought to myself, "Will I have a boring or a marvelous lunch?" I smiled to myself. Indeed I had a great lunch with my dear friend who just came back from Singapore. She is also a wonderful story creator.

Are you a story creator? Are you going to derive satisfaction, contentment, excitement and enjoyment from your daily existence?

Are you a genuine story listener? Are you going to participate in other people's stories? Are you going to influence and help them to create an even more exciting story with a happy ending?

Life is your own experience and you are the creator of your own stories. I am sure that your story is exciting.

Rock Climbing

Rock climbing was my son's top choice to celebrate his 11th birthday. He was going to challenge himself as well as his friends.

His younger brother was not sure whether he should join the group. One hour before the party my friend called and asked if her 7-year-old could join the rock climbing party. My younger son heard our conversation. He decided to join the group also.

Climbing the 20 foot wall was an easy task for my older son. He conquered every single wall the instructor suggested. But it was a hard task for the other 11-year-old boys. One of them quit after he reached 5 feet, two of them quit after 10 feet. "It is too hard. It is too high. I am afraid of heights." The boys told others when they finally touched the floor.

My younger son followed in his older brother's footsteps. His legs were trembling. He struggled, rested and struggled again. With his family cheering him on, he finally reached the top. Then he struggled even harder to get down. He would not let go and slide down the wall.

I held the sweaty little one and asked him how he felt. He told me the same thing the other boys said, he was tired and scared. "Why didn't you quit?" I asked. "I saw the top. I was very close to it! My brother did it, I told myself, I can do it too!" he replied.

We all experience fear, a tiring moment, a feeling of unfair competition and treatment. Some of us quit because we do not have a goal or a hope for the outcome. Some of us continue because we have clear goals and faith in our success.

Motivate yourself if you Are Laid Off

I have talked to many friends who have lost their jobs in the recent economic downturn. Losing your job is sad in this shaky job market and I am amazed to discover what my friends are doing during their downtime. Here is a list of how some of them are putting their time to good use:

- Start a dream business, or provide advice to others

- Volunteer in their children's activities, become a coach

- Volunteer in non-profit organizations, help others

- Network with a positive attitude

- Write books and articles

- Explore long term goals and passions, put a plan together and start to execute the plan

- Exercise intensively

- Offer free services to companies that eventually turn into your clients

- Send resumes selectively and follow up diligently

By filling your life with some of the above activities, there is little time to be depressed. Accept the layoff and use your free time positively.

A friend recently shared his layoff experience with me. He lost his job a few months ago. He kept a positive attitude while building the following routine for his unexpected free time. He spent each morning at the library or in bookstores reading anything that interested him. He spent the afternoon working with his children on their homework and cooking dinner for his wife. He sent resumes to his friends and recruiters for interesting job openings that had great growth potential. He found a job he liked in three months. He told me he really enjoyed the jobless three months, when he enriched his knowledge and learned how to enjoy his family more. During his job interview, his positive attitude and updated knowledge stood out and won him a job he liked.

When my neighbor lost his job, he spent three months of his time in gyms. He lost 50 pounds and became fit and energetic. With his better health and high energy level, he found a good job. I see him jogging every day as I am out for my morning run.

It is time to get your brand refreshed! You might have an outdated brand because you worked for one company and on one job too long, or your job is offshored. If you spend some time to review what you have accomplished, you will be able to use tips from Chapter Four to redesign your professional brand. The good news is you have enough time to fill missing skill gaps. Recruiters love LinkedIn where they can find your updated profile, which is the highlight of your resume. They also like to know the recommendations from your professional network. LinkedIn is a brilliant platform which you should use to refresh your brand continuously.

When you are laid off, despite all the negative aspects of the layoff, you are given the most valuable gift – time. It is your decision on how to spend this fortune and what kind of outcome you obtain at the end of this temporary period.

Balance your Work and Life

"How can I balance my work with my life and keep myself motivated?" is the question I have been asked repeatedly at every talk, class and conference I have given. More women ask this question than men because of their additional roles as wives and mothers. Every working woman is constantly challenged and struggling between work and family. Many of them are on the verge of being burned out. Can we really overcome this challenge?

Yes, we can, by delegating, empowering and paying for help.

Behind every successful career, there must be someone who is quietly supportive. A few of my friends, very accomplished ladies, have stay-at-home husbands or full time nannies. My in-laws have lived with us since I was pregnant with my first child; they help with cooking and childcare. To reduce the amount of chores, I hire gardeners, cleaners, drivers and private teachers for my children. I use money to buy time and preserve my energy. Therefore, when I get back home, I can spend more quality time with my children.

When my children grew older, I found out that they were just as capable as I was at their ages. With YouTube and Google, they can cook what they like, even make dessert and some dishes for our Thanksgiving dinner. They feel we trust and empower them. My guests' praise lit up my children's proud faces.

Will your house, dinner and children be the same if you were staying home? Definitely not. That is the price you pay for your career. You have to be open-minded and realistic to manage everything.

I learned a lot from working mothers and successful career women about how to simplify their lives. One IBM executive, who is on frequent business trips, reserves 30 minutes daily on her calendar at 7 PM in her children's time zone. She always calls them even if it is 3 AM in her time zone. She speaks to her children about homework and what happens during their day. She bought 7 bags for each child, marked from Monday to Sunday. Her children put their clothes in each bag on Sunday after she finishes the laundry. When traveling, she always takes black pants and blazers and a few different colored shirts so she can travel light.

I like to wear suits because I can get myself ready and look very professional in 2 minutes in the morning. I like to read and answer my email while exercising on my elliptical; I have become very good at typing on the elliptical. If you are open-minded, you can discover many ways to balance your life and work, have a good family life and a successful career at the same time.

Tournament of Champions

My older son was an excellent baseball player. He was fast, strategic and calm under stress. In the summer of 2009, he was on a great team. They won the Saratoga AAA Little League Championship. The team advanced to the Regional Minor Tournament of Champions.

Everyone was excited. The coaches and team practiced every day.

They won the first game on Saturday. They won the 2nd game on Monday. They won the 3rd game on Tuesday. Then they entered the final. It was a tough game. Luck was not on our side. Many hits were caught in midair, there were two questionable calls from the umpires and the team got frustrated. My son scored but the team lost the game. They ended up in 2nd place.

The final game wiped out the joy from all recent victories. Everyone felt defeated instead of enjoying the great season. I know I was one of them.

My son and I walked to my car, I asked him, "How do you feel?" His face was still calm, showing neither excitement nor disappointment. "Mom, it is okay", he said. "I learned one thing from my coach: if you want it bad enough, use your heart and guts, you will get it eventually."

It was a moment of truth in my life. We use our

brains every day forgetting about our hearts and guts, the sources of true success. So gather your passion and courage and go for what you want in your life. Eventually you will get it.

Reward your Team

What can we do to keep the team motivated? Driving the team hard and timely rewards can be the best combination. Reward the team when they reach goals, making their success a long lasting memory and happy experience to be with each other. Rewards should extend to family members who support their long working hours and sacrifices. Rewards should be something that makes them proud and gives them a right to brag. Here are a few of my favorite ideas:

- Dinner for two

- Movie passes for employee's family

- Ski trips for employees and their families

- Team building activities such as hiking, bowling, cooking, boating, river rafting and watching movies

- An appreciation letter to their parents or someone who will be proud of them

- A small donation to their favorite charity

- A framed award ready to hang

- A free trip to the most popular vacation place for the outstanding employee's whole family

Small rewards distributed in a timely fashion keep your team interested in doing a good job. The very best, costing you almost nothing, award you can give is a sincere thank you, preferably in front of the group. Most companies give bonuses on a regular schedule, but these smaller awards along the way are inspiring to your staff.

The Next Step – Plan for Retirement

Many of our students know that Pat took an early retirement and she would like to share her successful retirement career with you below.

Although my early retirement offer came up very quickly, and I was still pretty young (44) to consider leaving the wonderful world of commerce, I actually was in a pretty good place when the offer came because I had been planning for retirement most of my career.

Planning for retirement should start on the same day you start working, at least the financial planning part. When you sign up for your 401k or IRA, you make decisions that will carry you into retirement. The compound interest you earn on money saved in your 20s and 30s will grow and help fund your retirement. That day comes a lot faster than you can ever conceive.

Have Something to Do When you Get Up in the Morning

When I told my mother I planned to retire early, she said, "You have to have something to do when you get up in the morning." It is important to think about what you want to do in the next phase in your life. That may mean you get another job. It may mean you plan to go back to school or do volunteer work. Whatever it is, you need to plan for it in the same way you planned for your career.

One thing I learned quickly when I retired is you stretch the chore to fit the time you have available. Something that took me an hour to do when I was working may be stretched into 2 or 3 days after I retired. Procrastinating and stretching projects turn into not doing them at all. Soon you have no reason to get up in the morning. You really have nothing to do, having nothing to do leads to feeling worthless. Eventually you do become lazy and you are not very proud of yourself. You think no one needs you and you become very self-centered. Soon you are sitting on the porch wondering why the world is not beating a path to your door begging you come out and play. Life is not much fun and you wait around to die. And then you do die.

Planning for the next step of your life is extremely important, both financially and mentally. Have your finances in order owing no one, if possible. Then think of all the wonderful things you will do in the next phase of your life. Plan what you will do the first day you wake up. Believe me; you will be much happier if you think about these things in advance. There are wonderful things to do now that you have more time to experience them.

Start a New Career

Many people take advantage of retirement, especially if it is an early retirement, to start a second career. Many professionals take all the information they learned while working and go into teaching, often at the college or university level. Others decide to go into business for themselves. Still others choose to go to college to learn how to start a new career or just to get the degree they never had the time to earn.

Volunteer and Give Back

Some people choose to give back to society and volunteer their time to help others. There are countless organizations that want and need volunteers. Surprisingly, many organizations could not succeed without volunteers. Here are some of them:

- Hospitals
- Public libraries
- Literacy organizations

- Schools – tutoring, aiding teachers, reading to children

- Local festivals – in Reno, Hot August Nights, Air Races, Balloon Races

- Retired Senior Volunteer Program (RSVP)

- City and county volunteers - law enforcement aids

- And many, many more

When I retired, I thought about all the things I had done when working and what I enjoyed the most. I decided it was teaching. I also have a life-long love of reading. So I decided to volunteer to teach adults to read, write and speak English. I took a class to become certified as English as a Second Language (ESL) tutor. Later I was asked to become certified to teach other volunteers to become tutors. Then I became certified to become a supervisory tutor trainer in both literacy and ESL, where I conducted workshops to certify tutor trainers.

This effort has brought me more joy than I could ever have envisioned. Many of my students became the children I never had and they rewarded me with grandchildren. I got to enjoy my children as adults, never having to change diapers or stay up all night rocking a colicky baby.

One does not volunteer to seek awards. However, they sometimes come your way. I have been recognized and rewarded with a number of awards for my efforts:

Locally:

- An Angel in the Flesh
- Valley of the Sierras Chapter of the International Association of Administrative Professionals

State:

- Vietnam Veterans of America for continuous support and service benefiting the inmates at the Nevada State Prison
- You Make the Difference – Literacy Awards
- AT&T Pioneers
- American Institute for Public Service – Jefferson Award

National:

- The President's Volunteer Service Award – USA Freedom Corps
- American Institute for Public Service – Jefferson Award – Jacqueline Kennedy Onassis Award for Public Service

I feel certain I will always be involved with literacy in some way.

Lifelong Learning

I am a strong believer in lifelong learning. I am convinced we start to die when we are no longer interested in learning new things. I joined Osher Lifelong Learning Institute (OLLI) at the University of Nevada, Reno. This is a program connected with a university in every state, for seniors, which fosters intellectual stimulation, new interests and personal development through academic pursuits and to provide a community in which to gather, get acquainted and socialize. There are lectures and groups and no tests! I have seen seniors grow and prosper. One 93-year old member told me, "OLLI keeps me alive." I say it not only keeps me alive, it keeps me interesting to be around.

There are lots of programs in all our communities available to seniors to keep themselves interested and interesting. Look around for them and check them out. My only rule at retirement has been, "If it is not fun, I'm not going to do it." I suggest you may want to adopt it too.

Homework

Discover the best way to reward yourself and others:

1.   List your emotions related to successful goals.

2.   List three things to which you are emotionally attached.

3.   List three kinds of favorite foods, drinks and sports.

4.   What motivates your team members? What is their favorite food?

5.   How can you reward the most important person in your life?

6.   How can you reward people who help you?

7.   What can you do to reward the person who contributed the most to your team?

8.   Review your personal savings plans. Be sure you are planning for retirement financially and emotionally.

Appendix

Recommended Reading List

- *7 Habits of Highly Effective People* – Stephen Covey

- *Leadership Engine: How Winning Companies Build Leaders at Every Level* – Noel M. Tichy, Eli B. Cohen

- *Attitude 101: What Every Leader Needs to Know* – John C. Maxwell

- *Influencer: The Power to Change Anything* – Kerry Patterson, Joseph Grenny, David Maxfield, Ron McMillan and Al Switzler

- *Articulate Executive: Learn to Look, Act, and Sound Like a Leader* – Granville Toogood

- *Hands off Manager: How to Mentor People and Allow Them to Be Successful* – Steve Chandler and Duane Black

- *Winning* – Jack Welch

- *Execution: The Discipline of Getting Things Done*- Larry Bossidy, Ram Charan, Charles Burck

- *Vital Friends* – Tom Rath

- *What Got you Here Won't Get you There* – Marshall Goldsmith

- Leadership Blog: www.Elizabethxu.com

About the Authors

Elizabeth Xu, Ph.D., High-tech executive, columnist, executive mentor, leadership speaker and Stanford Continuing Studies teaching faculty.

Elizabeth is the Senior Vice President (SVP) of Product Development at Rearden Commerce. Elizabeth drives Rearden's global software development, leading an innovative team of engineers to make smart web work for people. Prior to Rearden, Elizabeth served as SVP of software development at RMS and a partner at Business Innovation Services. Her career also includes nine years at Vitria Technology as SVP of product development and corporate officer, as well as Product Development manager at IBM, where she was on the original team to develop the IBM Content Management Suite. In recent years, Elizabeth devoted her time to elevating leadership skills in the technical community. Her well-received presentation "Ten Steps to a Successful Career" provides building blocks for individuals who pursue meaningful careers. The workshop was offered as a class at Stanford University where she co-teaches with her mentor Ms. Pat Zimmerman.

Elizabeth holds a Ph.D. in Atmospheric Science and an M.S. in Computer Science from the University of Nevada, Reno. She has earned an M.S. in Atmospheric Science and a B.S. in Space Physics from Peking University.

Patricia Zimmerman, Jefferson and Kennedy Award winner, leadership mentor

Pat retired after a 26-year career in the telecommunications industry. She held management positions for Illinois Bell Telephone Company and AT&T. In 1990, Pat took an early retirement and moved to Reno, Nevada. The next years of her life were spent in volunteer work on political campaigns, teaching adults to read, write, and speak the English language and helping to expand Osher Lifelong Learning Institute (OLLI) at the University of Nevada, Reno. She was on the OLLI Board of Directors for five years holding the positions of Vice President, President and Past President. She is a certified Supervisory Trainer for ProLiteracy America and conducts workshops teaching other volunteers to train and tutor adults. She has been Elizabeth's mentor since early 1992 and occasionally conducts workshops and presentations with her.

The American Institute for Public Service has recognized Pat for her accomplishments with the national awards, the Jefferson Award and the Jacqueline Kennedy Onassis Award for outstanding service.

Other awards include: Outstanding Trainers Award presented by the Nevada Literacy Coalition, "An Angel in the Flesh" award for community service by the Unity Church of Reno, the President's Volunteer Service Award from the President's Council on Service and the Vietnam Veterans of America recognized her for civic participation and continuous support and service.

Made in the USA
Middletown, DE
26 June 2015